PRESENTED TO:

_____

BY:

_____

DATE:

_____

QUIET MOMENTS
WITH GOD
FOR COUPLES

Honor Books
Tulsa, Oklahoma

Quiet Moments with God for Couples
ISBN 1-56292-666-7
45-253-00242
Copyright © 2002 by Honor Books
P.O. Box 55388
Tulsa, Oklahoma 74155

INTRODUCTION

*Q*uiet moments—for personal meditation, for time together as a couple, for fellowship with God—we all need them, and we need them all on a regular basis.

Our world is moving and swirling past us with great speed and intensity. It's tempting to put those quiet times aside and regard them as luxuries rather than necessities. But the truth is—moments of quiet tranquility are critical. They help us define our relationships, our priorities, and ourselves. Without them, we become slaves to our lifestyles rather than the masters of them.

We hope you will find that the devotionals in this book help to make your quiet moments productive and inspiring. We have selected those that relate specifically to the issues couples face. And we have made them short enough to fit easily into your special time together, yet long enough to provide a solid kick-off for your day. As you read, we hope that they will draw you closer to each other and closer to God.

LIKE THE FIRST MORNING

What a joy it must have been for the first man and woman to awaken in the morning just after their creation!

Before them lay a beautiful garden without blemish, a harmonious creation without turmoil, an orderly environment without so much as a weed or thorn. Most wonderful of all, they freely walked and talked with the Lord in the cool of the day. Wouldn't you love to experience that glorious state of being for just one morning!

Eleanor Farjeon must have felt the same elation when she penned the words to her now internationally famous hymn:

> Morning has broken like the first morning;
> Blackbird has spoken like the first bird.
> Praise for the singing! Praise for the morning!
> Praise for them, springing fresh from the Word!
>
> Sweet the rain's new fall sunlit from heaven,

FOR THE LORD IS GOOD AND HIS LOVE ENDURES FOREVER; HIS FAITHFULNESS CONTINUES THROUGH ALL GENERATIONS..

PSALM 100:5

Like the first dew-fall on the first grass.
Praise for the sweetness of the wet garden,
Spring in completeness where his feet pass.

Mine is the sunlight! Mine is the morning
Born of the one light Eden saw play!
Praise with elation, praise every morning,
God's recreation of the new day![1]

While we may not awaken to a perfect, pristine world in our natural bodies, we *can* awaken to a "brand-new day" in our minds and hearts. We can walk and talk with the Lord all day long. Each day the Lord presents to His beloved children wondrous possibilities to explore with Him.

Let us always remember that He is the *Creator* and our loving Father. No matter what state we find ourselves in, He can create something new in us, for us, and through us. What cause for praise! His next act of creation is waiting to unfold as we yield our life to Him this morning and throughout our day!

LOVE IS A REFRESHING
BREEZE THROUGH THE
WINDOWS OF THE HEART.

CHERIE RAYBURN

First Cup

Many people wouldn't dream of starting their day without a cup of coffee. They count on that "first cup of the day" to wake them up and get them going.

There are others who have discovered an even more potent day-starter: first-thing-in-the-morning prayer.

For some, this is a prayer voiced to God before getting out of bed. For others, it is a planned time of prayer between getting dressed and leaving for work. For still others, it is a commitment to get to work half an hour early to spend quiet, focused time in prayer before the workday begins.

Henry Ward Beecher, one of the most notable preachers of the last century, had this to say about starting the day with prayer:

In the morning, prayer is the key that opens to us the treasure of God's mercies and blessings. The first act of the soul in early morning should be a draught at the heavenly fountain. It will sweeten the taste for the day.

. . . And if you tarry long so sweetly at the throne, you will come out of the closet as the high priest of Israel came from the awful ministry at the altar of incense, suffused all over with the heavenly fragrance of that communion.[2]

A popular song in Christian groups several years ago read, "Fill my cup, Lord; I lift it up, Lord. Come and quench this thirsting of my soul. Bread of heaven, feed me till I want no more; Fill my cup, fill it up and make me whole."[3]

Morning prayer is a time to have your cup filled to overflowing with peace. Then, as you have contact with other people at home and at work, you can pour that same peace into them. And the good news is—unlimited free refills are readily available any time your cup becomes empty throughout the day!

WITHOUT PRAYER, NO WORK IS WELL BEGUN.

BOOK OF WISDOM

THE MORNING SACRIFICE

*T*he Levites were never given the option to skip morning devotions. They were *commanded* to keep the morning sacrifice every day, without exception. As part of the morning ritual in the Temple, the high priest had these three duties:

1. to trim the lamps, making sure each oil cup of the menorah had sufficient oil and that the wicks were properly positioned,

2. to burn sweet incense on the incense altar,

3. and to burn the fat of the "peace" offerings.

Once a week, as part of the morning ritual, the priest replaced the "shewbread" that was on constant display before the Lord.

The priest performed these functions in silent worship, wearing a highly symbolic vestment. As he worked, the only sound was the light tinkling of the bells on the hem of his garment.

THEIR DUTY WAS . . . TO STAND EVERY MORNING TO THANK AND PRAISE THE LORD.

1 CHRONICLES 23:28,30 NKJV

This ancient ritual may seem strange and of little meaning to us today, but one great lesson we can draw from it is this: the morning sacrifice involved *all* of the senses and the mind. The priest stood before the Lord with his identity clearly displayed; he stood before the Lord for examination.

His sacrifices touched upon all aspects of his humanity: The lamps symbolized his need for light—the ability to see with spiritual eyes. The incense was a picture of his need to dwell in an atmosphere infused with God's holy presence. The peace offerings were a sign of his need for peace with God and his fellow man. And the "shewbread" demonstrated his need for daily provision, which only the Lord could provide.

This was a ceremony that, in its silence, spoke clearly: "We need You. Without You, we have no life, no wholeness, no meaning."

We may not have a ritual to follow in our morning devotional times, but we must come before the Lord with the same spirit of dependency and obedience. The day ahead of us is not ours. Our lives belong to God. (See 1 Corinthians 6:20.)

Everything we need, He will supply. The day is His, even as we are His.

I THINK THAT IF EVER A MORTAL HEARD THE VOICE OF GOD IT WOULD BE IN A GARDEN AT THE COOL OF THE DAY.

F. FRANKFORT MOORE

STRAIGHT AHEAD

*T*he sun is barely up, and that annoying alarm clock is blaring in your ear. Groggily you reach over and fumble around until you hit the snooze button. *Just a few more minutes,* you think, *and then I can get up and face the day.*

The alarm sounds again. You know you can't put it off any longer. It's time to face the inevitable. It's time to wrestle another day to the ground.

After a couple of cups of coffee, your brain is finally humming. Now the question is, which of today's tasks should you tackle first? Before you begin your work, you might seek inspiration from this prayer, written by Jacob Boehme, a German shoemaker who was born more than four hundred years ago:

IT IS GOD WHO ARMS ME WITH STRENGTH AND MAKES MY WAY PERFECT.

2 SAMUEL 22:33

Rule over me this day, O God, leading me on the path of righteousness. Put your Word in my mind and your Truth in my heart, that this day I neither think nor feel anything except what is good and honest. Protect me from all lies and falsehood, helping me to discern deception wherever I meet it. Let my eyes always look straight ahead on the road you wish me to tread, that I might not be tempted by any distraction. And make my eyes pure, that no false desires may be awakened within me.[4]

A day without distractions, focused only on the important.

A day viewed through pure eyes.

A day marked by goodness and honesty.

A day of clear direction and no deception.

A day without falsehood and lies.

A day in which God's Word rules our minds and His truth reigns in our hearts.

Now that's a day worth getting up for! That's a day worth embracing fully, from the first second.

> GIVE WHAT YOU HAVE. TO SOMEONE, IT MAY BE BETTER THAN YOU DARE THINK.
>
> HENRY WADSWORTH LONGFELLOW

Morning People

*G*od made both the day and the night, and He called both of them good. It seems God also made "morning people," who have their greatest energy level in the morning, and "night people" who are most productive in the late hours. Let's look at some of the joys of being a morning person.

God promised the children of Israel they would see the glory of the Lord in the morning (Exodus 16:7). This promise came to them when they were hungry and in need of bread to eat. God supplied manna every morning until they reached the Promised Land. Like the children of Israel, we, too, can see the glory of the Lord when we seek Him in His Word. Each morning He provides the nourishment we need for the day.

Another blessing of morning time is it often brings an end to suffering and sadness (Psalm 30:5). Each day brings us a new opportunity to seek God for a fresh perspective on the problems and needs in our lives. When we give every minute and every circumstance of each day to the Lord, we can expect to see His light dawning throughout our day.

There are many examples in Scripture about people who rose early to meet God or to be about doing His will, among them Abraham, Moses, Joshua, Gideon, Job, and even Jesus. The Gospels tell us that Jesus went at dawn to teach the people who gathered in the temple courts.

The most glorious event of Christianity—the Resurrection—occurred in the early morning. Each morning we can celebrate Jesus' Resurrection as we watch the light of the day dispel the darkness of night.

START YOUR MORNING WITH GOD; HE'S BEEN UP ALL NIGHT WAITING FOR YOU!

UNKNOWN

WORKING TOGETHER

Toyohiko Kagawa was a noted Japanese poet and Christian social reformer. Although he suffered poor health, he lived among the needy in the slums and worked tirelessly to overcome social injustice. His poem, "Work," speaks of the source of his strength:

Work

AS GOD'S
PARTNERS WE
BEG YOU NOT
TO TOSS ASIDE
THIS
MARVELOUS
MESSAGE OF
GOD'S GREAT
KINDNESS.

2 CORINTHIANS
6:1 TLB

I *shall not say*
That I am busy—
Those who would help
The troubled people
Should expect to be
Busy always.
Christ was so thronged
By multitudes
He had no time to eat.
He said,
"To him that hath
Shall be given;
And from him that hath not
Shall be taken away
Even that
He seems to have."

Which means
That if we do not use
All of our powers
We lose them. . . .
Then, too, the problem is
To do our work
With all our hearts;
We do not tire
Of doing what we love.
But most of all,
Our strength and comfort come
Only when God
Dwells in our souls
Working together with us.[5]

No matter what work you do today, you will work with purpose and strength if God is your Partner. He is always with you, waiting for you to simply ask for His strength to finish the job!

WE LIVE IN DEEDS, NOT YEARS,
IN THOUGHTS, NOT BREATHS.

PHILLIP JAMES BAILEY

Take Your Time

*F*rank was like many Christians. He had been taught that if he truly wanted God to guide his steps each day, he should spend time with Him first thing every morning. He found a copy of a "Through the Bible in One Year" plan and got down to business: three chapters each morning and two each night.

Somehow though, the inspiration he expected to discover escaped him. He discussed the problem with his friend Carl. Frank said, "I wasn't sure how I would find the time to read the Bible every morning, but I manage to squeeze it in. Sometimes I have to rush through the chapters a little, but I always remember what I've read. You could quiz me on it, and I'd get an 'A.' So why do I feel as if I haven't really read it?"

I DELIGHT IN YOUR DECREES; I WILL NOT NEGLECT YOUR WORD.

PSALM 119:16

Carl answered, "It sounds to me as if you're reading the Bible the way you would a textbook. If you want to get into the meaning behind the words, pray before you read, and ask God to reveal things to you. Instead of looking at the

Bible as a reading assignment, think of it as a special meeting time with God—time you set aside to sit down and hear what He has to say to you."

"I get it," Frank said. "I was doing the old 'what's in it for me?' and expecting God to reward me for putting in the time."

"Give yourself more time to read and study," Carl suggested. "Even a few extra minutes can make a big difference. Just remember: the more time you give to God, the more time He gives back to you. Your day will go much better if you let *Him* set the pace and listen for what *He* has to say."

While it is important to read the Scriptures daily, it is far more important to read *until you sense in your spirit that God has said something to YOU*. Don't be concerned about reading a specific number of verses or chapters. The key is to read with a listening ear.

A LOT OF KNEELING KEEPS YOU
IN GOOD STANDING WITH GOD.

UNKNOWN

THE "TO-BE LIST"

> WHEN THE HOLY SPIRIT CONTROLS OUR
> LIVES HE WILL PRODUCE THIS KIND OF
> FRUIT IN US: LOVE, JOY, PEACE, PATIENCE,
> KINDNESS, GOODNESS, FAITHFULNESS,
> GENTLENESS AND SELF-CONTROL.
>
> GALATIANS 5:22-23 TLB

*N*early all of us face our day with a "to-do list." The Scriptures compel us, however, to have a "to-be list."

While it may be important to accomplish certain tasks, engage in certain projects, or have certain encounters during a day, what is more important *for eternity* is the person we *are* throughout the day.

From a "to-do" perspective, we tend to come before the Lord and say, "This is my list, and this is my schedule. Please be with me, help me, and bless me."

From a "to-be" perspective, we might make these requests of the Lord:

- Help me to reflect Your love today.
- Help me to display Your joy.
- Help me to manifest Your peace.
- Help me to practice Your patience.
- Help me to express Your kindness.

- Help me to make known Your goodness.
- Help me to reveal Your faithfulness.
- Help me to show Your gentleness.
- Help me to exhibit Your self-control.

Wishful thinking does not produce these traits, however. They come from a life lived in communication with the Lord. They are the distinguishing marks of His presence in our lives. Our "to-be" list, therefore, must always begin with an invitation to the Holy Spirit to inspire us and impel us toward good works.

In order to *express* the Lord's kindness, for example, we first must see ourselves as *receiving* the Lord's kindness. In receiving His kindness, we become much more attuned to opportunities in which we might show His kindness to others. "Being kind" becomes a part of everything we do. The way we do our chores, hold our meetings, run our errands, and engage in our projects displays His kindness to those around us.

A GOOD DEED IS NEVER
LOST: HE WHO SOWS
COURTESY REAPS FRIENDSHIP;
AND HE WHO PLANTS
KINDNESS GATHERS LOVE.

SAINT BASIL

No Darkness Here!

*O*nce upon a time a Cave lived under the ground, as caves have the habit of doing. It had spent its lifetime in darkness.

One day it heard a voice calling to it, "Come up into the light; come and see the sunshine."

THE PATH OF THE JUST IS LIKE THE SHINING SUN, THAT SHINES EVER BRIGHTER UNTO THE PERFECT DAY.

PROVERBS 4:18 NKJV

But the Cave retorted, "I don't know what you mean. There isn't anything but darkness." Finally the Cave was convinced to venture forth. He was amazed to see light everywhere and not a speck of darkness anywhere. He felt oddly warm and happy.

Turnabout was fair play and so, looking up to the Sun, the Cave said, "Come with me and see the darkness."

The Sun asked, "What is darkness?"

The Cave replied, "Come and see!"

One day the Sun accepted the invitation. As it entered the Cave it said, "Now show me your darkness." But there was no darkness!

The Apostle John opens his Gospel account by describing Jesus as the Word and as the Light—"the true light that gives light to every man" (John 1:9). It is John who also records Jesus proclaiming, "I am the light of the world. Whoever follows me will never walk in darkness, but will have the light of life" (John 8:12).

Jesus made this statement at the close of a feast, just as giant candelabra were being extinguished throughout the city of Jerusalem. During the feast these lamps had illuminated the city so that night seemed to be turned to day. "My light is *not* extinguishable," Jesus was saying, "regardless of the times or seasons."

As this day begins, remember that you take the Light of the World with you; wherever you go and regardless of what may happen during your day, His light cannot be put out.

THIS LITTLE LIGHT OF MINE,
I'M GONNA LET IT SHINE.

CHILDREN'S HYMN

EVERYDAY BENEFITS

*B*lessings we take for granted are often forgotten. Yet every day God "loads us with benefits." This morning think of some common things you may have taken for granted—and thank God for them:

- Lungs that work well and steadily—ten to fifteen times each minute
- Bones that protect vital organs and muscles to hold the bones in their place
- A healthy disease-fighting immune system
- An untiring heart that pumps nine pints of blood through a 60,000-mile network of vessels
- A body temperature that remains constant
- Our five senses—eyes to see the dawn, ears to hear your loved one's voice, a nose to smell the freshness of the early dew, the sense of touch to enjoy a hug, and the sense of taste to savor breakfast
- Nerve cells that synapse and send messages to other parts of the body
- A digestive system that brings nourishment to all the cells of the body

BLESSED BE THE LORD, WHO DAILY LOADS US WITH BENEFITS.

PSALM 68:19 NKJV

- The ability—and desire—to get up and out of bed in the morning
- A place to live and a place to work
- Loving and supportive family, friends, and colleagues and the opportunities to let them know you care about them
- An intimate relationship with God through Jesus Christ
- The changing seasons that remind us of the different times of our lives
- Each day's unique beauty—the angle of the sun, white clouds stretched out across the blue afternoon sky, the gold and pink sunset
- The rotation of the earth that gives us day and night
- Times for quiet reflection and grateful remembrances
- The gift of laughter—and the ability to laugh at our mistakes

Add your own blessings to this list, and keep it growing all day long![6]

WHAT YOU ARE IS GOD'S GIFT
TO YOU. WHAT YOU MAKE OF
YOURSELF IS YOUR GIFT TO GOD.

UNKNOWN

LOVE AND FAITHFULNESS

PROCLAIM YOUR LOVE IN THE MORNING
AND YOUR FAITHFULNESS AT NIGHT.

PSALM 92:2

The psalmist encourages us to proclaim the Lord's love in the morning.

This proclamation of love is not a matter of our echoing Elizabeth Barrett Browning in saying to the Lord, "How do I love thee? Let me count the ways." Our love is not a recitation of the reasons why God is worthy of our love. Nor is it a declaration of our love for Him. Rather, our proclamation of love is to be a statement of how the Lord loves us!

How *does* He love us?

As you meditate on the Lord's love for you, certain words come to mind. Certainly the Lord loves you unconditionally . . . gently . . . individually . . .intimately . . . eternally . . . closely . . . warmly . . . tenderly . . . kindly. You are His child. He always has your good in mind. The Apostle Paul said of God's love:

Who shall separate us from the love of Christ? . . . For I am persuaded that neither death nor life, nor angels nor principalities nor powers, nor things present nor things to come, nor height nor depth, nor any other created thing, shall be able to separate us from the love of God which is in Christ Jesus our Lord.

—ROMANS 8:35,38-39 NKJV

Proclaiming the Lord's love for you in the morning will give you strength. Because you have a loving Father with you always, you can make it through any day, regardless of the surprises—good and bad—that come your way.

After beginning and walking through your day in God's love, at the day's end you can easily recount *His faithfulness*. He is faithful to provide what you need, deliver you from evil, and lead you into blessings—all of which are expressions of His love. In recognizing God's love first and foremost, and then living in that love all day long, you quickly recognize the *power* of God's love to sustain you, energize you, and protect you—and you give that love to others.

This morning, accept and expect the Lord to be loving toward you . . . and by tonight, you will surely *know* He has been faithful!

FAITHFULNESS IS CONSECRATION IN OVERALLS.

EVELYN UNDERHILL

TRUE IDENTITY

*E*very day the world challenges your identity by trying to tell you who you are—or ought to be—by shaping your desires and by telling you what is important, what values you should have, and how to spend your time and resources. What the world is telling you may not be true!

The story is told of a rancher who had been hunting in the mountains of West Texas. Up high on a cliff he came across an eagle's nest. He took one of the eagle's eggs back to his ranch and placed it under one of his hens sitting on her eggs. Eventually the eagle's egg hatched. The mother hen took care of the eaglet along with her baby chicks who hatched at the same time.

The eagle made its home in the barnyard along with the chickens. It ate, slept, and lived just like the chickens. One day an eagle from the nearby mountain swooped down over the barnyard in search of prey. Trying to get her chicks and the eaglet to safety, the mother hen squawked loudly.

As the great eagle swooped low across the barnyard, he also let out a harsh scream—a scream made only by eagles. The young chicks heeded their mother's warning, but the eaglet responded to the call of the eagle. He took flight and ascended, following the eagle to the mountain heights.

What does Scripture tell us about who we are as children of God? We are the apple of His eye (Zechariah 2:8); the flock of His people (Zechariah 9:16); a crown of glory in the hand of the Lord and a royal diadem in the hand of your God (Isaiah 62:3); the temple of God (1 Corinthians 3:16). We are heirs of God and joint heirs with Christ (Romans 8:17). We are kings and priests of our God (Revelation 5:10). We were created to bear His likeness (Genesis 1:27).

Most importantly, we are God's children (1 John 3:1). We belong to Him, and our hearts cry, "Abba, Father!" when He calls to us.

Listen for His call today! Find out who you are and what your purpose is from Him, the One who made you!

> THE MAN WITHOUT A PURPOSE IS
> LIKE A SHIP WITHOUT A RUDDER—
> A WAIF, A NOTHING, A NO MAN.
>
> THOMAS CARLYLE

NEVER GIVE UP

*F*ire is a gift—of warmth, light, beauty, and utility. Nothing beats a crackling fire on a cold winter's night, and who hasn't enjoyed roasting marshmallows over an open fire? But fire also can be an enemy. Sometimes it destroys the things we love.

On January 29, 1996, a blaze consumed one of Venice's most treasured buildings: the 204-year-old opera house, La Fenice. Hundreds of Venetians stood and watched as the building went up in flames.

Cause for sadness? Definitely. Cause for despair? Absolutely not. The construction of La Fenice had been delayed by fire in 1792. Another fire in 1836, had forced the Venetians to rebuild. And so, too, after the fire in 1996, Venetians are already rallying to rebuild their opera house.

Interestingly, *La Fenice* means "the phoenix," referring to the mythological Egyptian bird that died in a fiery nest, only to emerge

FORGETTING WHAT IS BEHIND AND STRAINING TOWARD WHAT IS AHEAD, I PRESS ON TOWARD THE GOAL TO WIN THE PRIZE FOR WHICH GOD HAS CALLED ME HEAVENWARD IN CHRIST JESUS.

PHILIPPIANS 3:13-14

from the ashes as a brand-new bird. It is in that spirit that the Venetians rebuild.

Can we restore what the fires in our lives destroy? Sometimes. If we desire to rebuild and we truly believe it is what the Lord would have us do, we put our full effort into the task. At other times when the Lord brings us through a fire, His desire is for the old to be left in ashes so something entirely *different* can be constructed on the site. This is true not only in the physical world in which we live, but also in the interior world of our souls, when our inner mettle is "tried by fire."

In those cases when we can't or shouldn't rebuild, we can remember Shadrach, Meshach, and Abednego. They were thrown into Nebuchadnezzar's fiery furnace for refusing to bow to an idol. (See Daniel, chapter 3.) Like them, we can emerge stronger and better after having been tested. We can see our lives touch and inspire others when we stand up for what we believe.

If you are facing calamity or disaster today, the Bible tells you to quickly put it behind you by rebuilding or building something new. Whichever God desires, you will become stronger and better than before if you "press on!"

THE JOURNEY OF A THOUSAND MILES
MUST BEGIN WITH A SINGLE STEP.

LAO-TZE

THE PEOPLE FACTOR

"GREATER LOVE HATH NO MAN
THAN THIS, THAT A MAN LAY
DOWN HIS LIFE FOR HIS FRIENDS."

JOHN 15:13 KJV

Wanted: Someone willing to risk his or her life to rescue 200 Jewish artists and intellectuals from the Nazis. Faint of heart need not apply.

Would you jump at the chance to take on this job? Varian Fry did. A high-school Latin teacher from Connecticut, he went to Marseilles, France, in August 1941, intending to stay only three weeks. He stayed fourteen months.

Forging passports and smuggling people over the mountains into Spain, Fry and a handful of American and French volunteers managed to save almost 4,000 people from the Nazi scourge. Among them were the 200 well-recognized Jewish artists and intellectuals he originally intended to rescue.

Did Fry have a difficult time motivating himself each day to face the task in front of him? Probably not. He had little doubt what he was doing had divine purpose and tremendous significance.

Most of us will never find ourselves in Fry's position, and often we wonder if what we do throughout our day has any significance at all. In many cases, it takes more strength to do the trivial tasks than the monumental ones.

If the job we do is difficult, we must ask God to show us how to make the task less strenuous. If the job is dull, we need to ask God to reveal ways to make it more interesting. If we think our work is unimportant, we need to remember that being in God's will and doing a good job for Him will not only bring blessing to others, but also blessing to us, both now and for eternity.

Often it is the *people* factor that keeps us motivated. God gives us purpose and makes our lives meaningful, but He is always working to bless us so we can turn around and bless other people.

The tasks you face today are significant as you work to meet a need or to see growth in others. You will see God's love moving through your life to others in everything you do for them—from putting a bandage on a child's skinned knee to inventing a machine which helps people with asthma breathe.

NO ONE IS USELESS IN THIS
WORLD WHO LIGHTENS
THE BURDEN OF ANOTHER.

CHARLES DICKENS

THE GIVING FACTOR

*M*uch of our day is spent in getting. We *get* up in the morning in order to *get* a good breakfast before we *get* a ride to work. We *get* in gear and *get* the job done so we can *get* a paycheck that will pay for a *get*away on the weekend so we might *get* rest to *get* a jump on the coming week!

"GIVE, AND IT WILL BE GIVEN TO YOU; GOOD MEASURE, PRESSED DOWN, SHAKEN TOGETHER, RUNNING OVER."

LUKE 6:38 NASB

The Gospel challenges us to become people who are more concerned about giving than getting. Giving sounds noble, and we instinctively know it's the "right thing to do," but in practice, giving is difficult. Genuine giving involves concern for others, and ultimately it requires the demolition of pride and self-centeredness. Giving is a sacrifice, letting go of at least part of that which we believe to be "ours."

The great mystery is that in giving, we get. What we get may not be what we had originally intended to get. Yet those who are generous in their giving repeatedly say that what they get in return is always far more valuable and meaningful than what they gave or what they had originally intended to get.

Norman Vincent Peale once said:

> The man who lives for himself is a failure. Even if he gains much wealth, position, or power, he is still a failure. The man who lives for others has achieved true success. A rich man who consecrates his wealth and his position to the good of humanity is a success. A poor man who gives of his service and his sympathy to others has achieved true success, even though material prosperity or outward honors never come to him.

Find a way to give *something* to someone in need today, whether of your money, time, talent, effort, service, tears, laughter, ideas, or possessions. Give freely and generously, not motivated by a payback. The payback will come, but let its arrival be a joyful surprise in your day!

AS THE PURSE IS EMPTIED
THE HEART IS FILLED.

VICTOR HUGO

JIGSAW PUZZLE

*A*re you a jigsaw puzzle afficionado?

LOOKING AWAY
[FROM ALL THAT
WILL DISTRACT]
TO JESUS, WHO
IS THE LEADER
AND THE
SOURCE OF OUR
FAITH [GIVING
THE FIRST
INCENTIVE FOR
OUR BELIEF]
AND IS ALSO
ITS FINISHER
[BRINGING IT TO
MATURITY AND
PERFECTION].

HEBREWS 12:2 AMP

If you have ever worked complicated jigsaw puzzles, you know three things about them:

First, they take time. Few people can put several hundred pieces of a puzzle together rapidly. Most large and complex puzzles take several days, even weeks, to complete. The fun is in the *process,* the satisfaction in the *accomplishment.*

Second, the starting point of a puzzle is usually to identify the corners and edges, the pieces with a straight edge.

Third, jigsaw puzzles are fun to work by oneself, but even more fun to work with others. When a "fit" is discovered between two or more pieces, the excitement is felt by all the participants.

Consider the day ahead of you like a piece in the jigsaw puzzle of your life. Indeed, its shape is likely to be just as jagged, its colors just as unidentifiable. The meaning of today may *not* be sequential to that of yesterday.

What you experience today may actually *fit* with something you experienced several months ago, or something you will experience in the future. You aren't likely to see the big picture of your life by observing only one day. Even so, you can trust that there is a plan and purpose. All the pieces will come together according to God's design and timetable.

On some days, we find straight-edged pieces of our life's puzzle—truths that become a part of our reason for being. On other days, we find pieces that fit together so we understand more about ourselves and about God's work in our lives. And on all days, we can know the joy of sharing our lives with others and inviting them to be part of the process of discovering who we are.

The main thing to remember is to enjoy the process. Live today to the fullest, knowing one day you'll see the full picture.

LIFE IS WHAT WE MAKE IT, ALWAYS
HAS BEEN, ALWAYS WILL BE.

GRANDMA MOSES

ACTIVE FAITH

LET US NOT GIVE UP MEETING TOGETHER,
AS SOME ARE IN THE HABIT OF DOING,
BUT LET US ENCOURAGE ONE ANOTHER.

HEBREWS 10:25

*P*hilip Haille went to the little village of Le Chambon, France, to write about a people who, unlike other villages, had hidden their Jews from the Nazis. He wondered what caused them to risk their lives to do such extraordinary good.

He interviewed people in the village and was overwhelmed—not by their extraordinary qualities, but by their *ordinariness*. They were not an unusually bright, quick-witted, brave, or discerning people.

Haille looked for possible connections between the citizens' lives to find the reason they had done what no other French town had done. In the end, the author concluded that the one factor uniting them to do good was their attendance at their little church.

Sunday after Sunday they heard the sermons of Pastor Trochme. Over time they became people who knew what was right and obtained the courage from God to do it. When it came time for them to act boldly—as on the day the Nazis came to town—they quietly did what was right.

One elderly woman faked a heart attack when the Nazis came to search her house. She told Haille about her personal dramatic ploy, "Pastor always taught us that there comes a time in every life when a person is asked to do something for Jesus. When my time came, I just *knew* what to do."

There were two strong beliefs that gave the citizens of this town inner strength of steel. First, they knew their spiritual strength together in Christ was greater than any foe they faced. Even in times of war, they did not forsake gathering together. Second, they took the Word of God into their hearts in an active way—knowing God would bless them when the principles of their faith were reflected in their behavior.

The strength and courage Haille discovered in the people of Le Chambon was a result of their simple obedience to God—never to stop meeting together to worship and hear His Word. When extreme difficulty came their way, their unity in the faith was a habitual part of their everyday lives.

Thank God today for a church where you can receive strength and courage. If you don't go to church, ask the Lord to lead you to the body of believers just right for you.

STRENGTH AND HAPPINESS
CONSIST IN FINDING OUT
THE WAY GOD IS GOING, AND
GOING IN THAT WAY TOO.

HENRY WARD BEECHER

Perfect Combination

Sodium is an extremely active element that always links itself to another element.

Chlorine is a poisonous gas.

When combined, chlorine stabilizes sodium, and sodium neutralizes the poison of the chlorine.

The result, sodium chloride, is common table salt, a highly stable substance used through the centuries to preserve meat, enhance flavor, and, prior to modern medicine, help clean and heal wounds.

For a Christian, love and truth can be like sodium and chlorine. Both are essential elements in a believer's life, but pursuing one without the other can be unmanageable and even dangerous.

Love without truth is flighty, sometimes blind, and often willing

"YOU ARE THE SALT OF THE EARTH. BUT IF THE SALT LOSES IT SALTINESS, HOW CAN IT BE MADE SALTY AGAIN? IT IS NO LONGER GOOD FOR ANYTHING, EXCEPT TO BE THROWN OUT AND TRAMPLED BY MEN."

MATTHEW 5:13

to combine with strange or perverse doctrines. It is highly unstable, tossed to and fro on a sea of emotions.

On the other hand, truth by itself can be offensive, sometimes even poisonous. Spoken without love, it can turn people away from God. It can wound, even kill, a person's longing for the nurturing presence of the Heavenly Father.

When truth and love are combined in an individual or a church, however, we have what Jesus called "the salt of the earth." We are able to heal those with spiritual wounds, preserve and encourage the best in one another, and bring out the personal zest and unique gifts of each person.

Today as you deal with others, seek to let your words and actions be *grounded in truth* and *delivered with love.*

LOVE LOOKS NOT WITH THE
EYES, BUT WITH THE HEART.

WILLIAM SHAKESPEARE

LEADER OF THE PACK

*B*eing the owner of a small business is not easy. Just when you start to build a clientele, along comes a crafty competitor who copies your style or improves on your methods. Next thing you know, revenues are falling and you find yourself looking over your shoulder, trying to avoid being hit by another wave of wanna-bes.

THE FORMER THINGS HAVE TAKEN PLACE, AND NEW THINGS I DECLARE; BEFORE THEY SPRING INTO BEING I ANNOUNCE THEM TO YOU.

ISAIAH 42:9

A man on the West Coast found himself in this situation. His first venture was commercial fishing. When larger companies took over the water, he began renting out small sailboats and kayaks to people who wanted to explore the bay. Soon others with stronger financial backing moved in on that business.

Once again, he needed a new idea.

How about submarine tours? After doing some research, the entrepreneur realized the cost of buying and maintaining a sub was beyond his reach. But a semi-submersible underwater viewing boat was not! The boat looks like a sub, but it doesn't dive. Passengers can go below deck and view the fascinating world under the sea.[7]

When your income seems to be going out with the tide, you may need to be a little creative. Talk with other people, do some research, consider even the "crazy" ideas, and glean what you can from them. You never know which wave might be the one that carries you safely and profitably to the shore.

God's creative work didn't end with His creation of the world. He continues His work today by giving each of us a dose of creativity. He invites us to be part of His plan and purpose for the earth by using this creative energy. Your ideas are God's gift to you for your provision, prosperity, and the fulfillment of your purpose in life.

Ask the Lord to inspire you anew today. Ask Him to give you His next *idea* for your life!

WHATEVER YOU DO, OR
DREAM YOU CAN, BEGIN IT.

JOHANN WOLFGANG VON GOETHE

REMEMBERING GOD

CHOOSE FOR YOURSELVES THIS DAY WHOM YOU WILL SERVE.

JOSHUA 24:15

A rabbi once summoned the townsfolk to meet in the square for an important announcement. The merchants resented having to leave their businesses. The farmers could scarcely see how they could leave their fields. The housewives protested against leaving their chores. But obedient to the call of their spiritual leader, the townspeople gathered together to hear the announcement their teacher felt was so important to make at that time.

The rabbi said, "I wish to announce that there is a God in the world." And with that, he departed.

The people stood in silence—stunned, but not bewildered. They understood what he had said, with an understanding born of a heartfelt conviction. They realized they had been acting as if God did *not* exist. While they observed rituals and recited the correct order of prayers, their actions did not comply with the commandments of God. Their daily bread was sought and taken with little thought and reverence for Him.

We may not openly deny God, but instead we may try to confine Him to some remote corner of life. We keep Him away from our daily doings, associations, obligations, experiences, joys, heartaches, and all the commonplace things required to keep body and soul together. However, these are the facts:

- There is a God in the world you call your neighborhood.

- There is a God in the world you call your workplace.

- There is a God in the offices you frequent, the hospitals you visit, the airports through which you travel, the shops in which you make your purchases, and the dozens of places you walk in the course of a week.

There is a God . . . and He wants to be a part of *everything* you do.

Recognize He is with you *wherever* you go today. The knowledge that He is with you and that He is interested in every detail of your life will bring joy and peace to every experience.

YOU CAN NEVER DO A
KINDNESS TOO SOON, FOR
YOU NEVER KNOW HOW
SOON IT WILL BE TOO LATE.

RALPH WALDO EMERSON

THE SKY'S THE LIMIT

*P*eople are often afraid that commitment to Jesus Christ means an endless list of "don'ts" and "thou shalt nots."

Highly motivated personalities are especially vulnerable to the lie that God's ways will restrict their creativity and growth. They fear they may never reach their full potential if they are tied to a lot of religious restrictions.

"MY YOKE IS EASY, AND MY BURDEN IS LIGHT."

MATTHEW 11:30 KJV

Sadly, some of the smartest people on earth will never reach their full potential because they *aren't* tied to Jesus. The same holds for those who see His commands as "taking away all their fun." The fact is, true and lasting joy comes through knowing Jesus and following Him.

Consider this: You have watched a kite fly in the wind. Would you say the string that holds it is burdensome? No, it is there to control the kite. The kite will not fly unless it is in partnership with the string. The string and the kite are yoked together. You cannot cut the string and expect the kite to soar right up into the heavens. When the restrictive yoke of the string is cut, the kite may seem to fly freely for a moment, but it will soon crash to the ground.

The string gives the kite direction and purpose by sustaining its position against the wind and using the wind to its advantage. Without the string, the kite would be at the mercy of every passing influence and would doubtless end up being trapped in a tree or falling to the ground. When it is time for the kite to come to earth, the string gently reels it in, safely avoiding tree limbs and telephone poles.

In like manner, our daily surrender to the Lord Jesus is not burdensome, nor does it take away enjoyment in life. Like the kite string, He makes certain the wind is in our favor and we are always in position to get the most out of life.

Let Jesus be your "Kite String" today, and see if you don't fly higher!

A BURDEN SHARED IS A LIGHTER LOAD.

UNKNOWN

Taproots

The art of raising miniature trees, known as *bonsai*, was developed by the Japanese. To create a miniature tree, the taproot is cut, forcing the tree to live on only the nourishment provided by the little roots growing along the surface of the soil. The tree lives, but it does not grow. Trees dwarfed in this way reach a height of only twelve to eighteen inches.

The taproot of a tree is the part of the root system that goes deep into the soil to absorb essential minerals and huge quantities of water—sometimes several hundred quarts a day. Taproots grow deepest in dry, sandy areas where there is little rainfall. The root system of a tree not only nourishes the tree, but also provides stability, anchoring it securely into the ground so it cannot be blown over by strong winds.

THE ALMIGHTY ... BLESSES YOU WITH BLESSINGS OF THE HEAVENS ABOVE, BLESSINGS OF THE DEEP THAT LIES BELOW.

GENESIS 49:25

The root system is a good analogy for the Christian life. Richard J. Foster wrote, "Superficiality is the curse of our age. . . . The desperate need today is not for a greater number of intelligent people, or gifted people, but for deep people."

How do Christians grow deep in their spiritual life? In the same way a taproot grows deep—in search of the nourishment that will cause it to grow. In modern culture, Christians have to seek out spiritual food that will result in spiritual maturity. Regular times of prayer and Bible study, individual and corporate worship, servanthood, and Christian fellowship are just some of the ways Christians can grow deep roots.

What are the benefits of depth in our spiritual life? Like the tree . . .

- we will be able to stand strong—"the righteous cannot be uprooted"(Proverbs 12:3), and
- we will be fruitful—"the root of the righteous flourishes" (Proverbs 12:12).

Seek the Lord daily, so you can grow *deep* in your faith and withstand the storms of life.

> YOU CAN KEEP FAITH ONLY AS
> YOU CAN KEEP A PLANT, BY
> ROOTING IT INTO YOUR LIFE
> AND MAKING IT GROW THERE.
>
> PHILLIPS BROOKS

WHICH DAY PLANNER?

THE THINGS THAT I PURPOSE, DO I PURPOSE ACCORDING TO THE FLESH?

2 CORINTHIANS 1:17 KJV

*O*ne of the challenges of our busy lives today is to be organized, so we can "get it all done." There are a number of organizers and calendars available to help us schedule the precious hours of the day. Beepers and mobile telephones give us instant communication with anyone anywhere. We no longer get away from it all, because now we can take it all with us!

Sometimes we need to be challenged not to "get it all done," but to slow down and reflect on what it is we are trying to accomplish. We must be sure we are headed in the right direction with our families, work, church, community, and personal lives.

If we are not careful and prayerful, we may find ourselves agreeing with the modern-day philosopher who noted, "So what if you win the rat race—you are still a rat!"

God has a different "daily planner." The psalmist wrote about it in Psalm 105:

- Give thanks to the Lord.
- Call on His name.
- Make known among the nations what he has done.
- Sing to him, sing praise to him.
- Tell of all his wonderful acts.
- Glory in his holy name.
- Let the hearts of those who seek the Lord rejoice.
- Look to the Lord and his strength.
- Seek his face always.
- Remember the wonders he has done, his miracles, and the judgments he has pronounced.

Each day we have the privilege of consulting with the King of Kings and Lord of Lords to determine what path we will take, what tasks are most important, and who needs us the most.

YOU WILL NEVER "FIND"
TIME FOR ANYTHING.
IF YOU WANT TIME,
YOU MUST MAKE IT.

CHARLES BUXTON

A Shared Vision

*I*n *The Reasons of the Heart,* John S. Dunne writes eloquently:

> "There is a dream dreaming us," a Bushman once told Laurens Van der Post. "We are part of a dream, according to him, part of a vision. What is more, we can become aware of it." Although we are far removed from the Bushmen and their vision, it seems we can indeed come to a sense of being dreamed, being seen, being known. Our mind's desire is to know, to understand; but our heart's desire is intimacy, to be known, to be understood. To see God with our mind would be to know God, to understand God; but to see God with our heart would be to have a sense of being known by God, of being understood by God.
>
> If there is a dream dreaming us, it will be God's vision of us, and if we have a sense of

THE LORD HAS BEEN MINDFUL OF US; HE WILL BLESS US. . . . HE WILL BLESS THOSE WHO FEAR THE LORD, BOTH SMALL AND GREAT.

PSALMS 115:12-13

NKJV

being part of that dream, it will be our heart's vision of God.[8]

As we explore and encounter God's dream for us, we find our clearest and highest sense of identity and purpose in life, which gives us motivation and direction for each day.

Do you have a sense of God's vision for your life today? How does He see you? What does He desire for you? What does He dream of you doing, becoming, and being?

We know from His Word that God desires for you to be a person of character and quality, a person of noble and uncompromising virtue, a person of strength and spiritual power. He is calling you to a close, personal, and intimate relationship with Him. He eagerly desires to entrust you with His plans and desires for your life.

God has given you specific talents, abilities, spiritual gifts, and material endowments which He longs for you to use to their fullest. Purpose in your heart today to be His friend, His child, His heir, so that He can do what He loves to do—reward you with even greater blessings.

THE GREAT THING IN THIS WORLD IS NOT SO MUCH WHERE WE ARE, BUT IN WHAT DIRECTION WE ARE MOVING.

OLIVER WENDELL HOLMES

TODAY'S AGENDA

*O*ur days are hinged together in a unique way according to God's Word. Yesterday's pain, sorrow, and disappointment, as well as yesterday's victories and blessings, become today's agenda.

GIVING THEM A GARLAND INSTEAD OF ASHES, THE OIL OF GLADNESS INSTEAD OF MOURNING, THE MANTLE OF PRAISE INSTEAD OF A SPIRIT OF FAINTING, SO THEY WILL BE CALLED OAKS OF RIGHTEOUSNESS, THE PLANTING OF THE LORD, THAT HE MAY BE GLORIFIED.

ISAIAH 61:3 NASB

Were you rejected or alienated by someone yesterday? Then God's agenda for you today is one of restoration and reconciliation.

Were you struck with sickness or an injury yesterday? Then healing is on today's agenda.

Were you dealt a disappointment or handed a bad report? Then today is a day for hope and good news.

Were you struck with a calamity or disaster? Then today is the time for recovery and rejuvenation.

Did you fail in some way yesterday? Then God's agenda for you today is a second chance!

No matter what worry, frustration, or heartache you took with you to bed last night . . . today holds the hope for a reversal of that "trouble." This is the redemptive nature of God's work in our lives: turning our losses into victories, our sorrow into gladness, and our discouragement into reason for praise!

The prophet Isaiah tells us this process results in our becoming so firmly rooted in God's goodness we are like great "trees of righteousness." We grow to the point where we see no matter *what* may strike us on one day, the Lord has a plan for full recovery *and more* beginning the next. The Apostle Paul echoed this when he wrote to the Romans: "All things work together for good to those who love God, to those who are the called according to *His* purpose" (Romans 8:28 NKJV).

Our rebound is never back to the point where we began, but instead it always takes us higher. We are wiser and richer. No matter what hits us, our roots grow deeper, our branches grow longer, and our fruit is increased.

Expect God's turnabout in your life today!

THE GREAT PLEASURE IN LIFE IS DOING
WHAT PEOPLE SAY YOU CANNOT DO.

WALTER BAGEHOT

STAY THE COURSE

[JESUS] STEDFASTLY SET HIS FACE TO GO TO JERUSALEM.

LUKE 9:51 KJV

*T*he Saturday of the dog sled derby dawned as a bright, clear, cold winter morning. The people of the small Wisconsin town on the southern shore of Lake Superior looked forward to the annual competition. The one-mile course across the ice had been marked out by little fir trees set into the surface of the frozen lake. Spectators standing on the steep slope along the shore had a good view of the entire course.

The contestants were all children—ranging from large, older boys with several dogs and big sleds to one little guy who appeared to be no more than five years old. He entered the race with a little sled pulled by his small dog, and he lined up with the rest of the entrants waiting for the race to begin.

When the signal was sounded declaring the start of the race, the racers took off in a flurry, and the youngest contestant, with his little dog, was quickly outdistanced. In fact, the larger and more experienced racers disappeared so quickly down the course that the little guy was hardly in the race at all. The contest was going well, however, and even though in last place, the little fellow stayed in the competition, enjoying every minute.

About halfway around the course, the dog team that was in second began to overtake the team that was in the lead. The dogs came too close to the lead team, and soon the two teams were in a fight. Then, as each sled reached the fighting, snarling animals, they joined in the fracas.

None of the drivers seemed to be able to steer their teams clear of the growling brawl, and soon all of the dogs and racers became one big seething mass of kids, sleds, and dogs—all, that is, but the little fellow and his one dog. He managed to stay the course and was the only one to finish the race.[9]

Each day holds the potential for something to sidetrack us from our intended purpose. No matter how great the distraction, we can finish the course if we stay focused and keep going!

ONE MAY GO WRONG IN
MANY DIRECTIONS, BUT
RIGHT IN ONLY ONE.

ARISTOTLE

AT LAST . . .

The story is told of a diamond prospector in Venezuela named Rafael Solano. He was one of many impoverished natives and fortune seekers who came to sift through the rocks of a dried-up riverbed reputed to have diamonds. No one, however, had had any luck for some time in finding any diamonds in the sand and pebbles. One by one, those who came left the site—their dreams shattered, and their bodies drained.

Discouraged and exhausted, Solano had just about decided it was time for him to give up too. He had nothing to show for months of hard work.

Then he stooped down one last time and scooped up a handful of pebbles, if only so he could say he had personally inspected every pebble in his claim. From the pebbles in his hand, he pulled out one that seemed a little different. He weighed it in his other hand. It seemed heavy. He measured it and weighed it on a scale. Could it be?

Sure enough, Solano had found a diamond in the rough! New York jewelry dealer Harry Winston paid

> I WILL PRAISE YOU, FOR YOU HAVE ANSWERED ME, AND HAVE BECOME MY SALVATION.
>
> PSALM 118:21 NKJV

Solano $200,000 for that stone. When it was cut and polished, it became known as the Liberator, and it is considered the largest and purest unmined diamond in the world.

You may have been plugging away at a project for weeks, even months or years, without seeing much progress. Today may be the day. Don't give up!

The Scriptures are filled with examples of men and women who, on the verge of disaster or failure, experienced God's creative work in their lives. Remind yourself of the following things:

- God's Word is true.
- God can part the sea.
- God can heal the incurable.
- God can provide water from a rock and manna from the heavens.
- God can conquer your enemies.
- God can still deliver from the fiery furnace and the lion's den.

Persevere in what He has asked you to do today because your rewards will be more than you can think or imagine!

> ## THE FRUITS OF LABOR ARE THE SWEETEST OF ALL PLEASURES.
>
> MARQUIS DE VAUVENARGUES

A SOARING IMAGINATION

*I*n his classic self-help book *Think & Grow Rich,* Napoleon Hill wrote, "Whatever the mind of man can conceive and believe, he can achieve." His premise, and that of many others, is that once the human mind has been programmed with a certain expectation, it will begin to act to fulfill that expectation.

The Scriptures declared this principle long before Hill wrote his book. Faith is believing and then seeing. It is expecting a miracle before receiving a miracle.

> FAITH IS THE SUBSTANCE OF THINGS HOPED FOR, THE EVIDENCE OF THINGS NOT SEEN.
>
> HEBREWS 11:1 NKJV

The Aluminum Company of America coined an interesting word: *imagineering.* They combined the idea of imagining a product or service, with the idea that this dream could then be engineered into a reality. Throughout history we've seen this principle at work:

- Our primitive ancestors came up with the idea that it was easier to roll objects than drag them—and they carved a wheel from stone.

- A man named Gutenberg imagined that letters might be set in metal and combined to create words, which then could be printed repeatedly with the application of ink. He set about to make such a machine.

- People designed cathedrals that took decades to build—but build them they did.

Your future will be impacted directly by the *ideas* and *dreams* that you have today. What you begin to believe for, and then how you act on that belief, will result in what you have, do, and are in the days, weeks, months, and years ahead.

Let your "faith imagination" soar today. Believe for God's highest and best in your life. And then begin to live and work as if that miracle is on its way.

TODAY WELL-LIVED MAKES
EVERY YESTERDAY A DREAM
OF HAPPINESS, AND EVERY
TOMORROW A VISION OF HOPE.

FROM THE SANSKRIT

THE VALUE OF ONE

"THERE IS JOY IN THE PRESENCE
OF THE ANGELS OF GOD OVER
ONE SINNER WHO REPENTS."

LUKE 15:10 NASB

*S*ome days it's hard just to get out of bed. Our motivation is either fading, or it's completely gone. We are overcome with a "What difference does it make?" attitude. We become overwhelmed at the immensity of the duties before us. Our talents and resources seem minuscule in comparison to the task.

A businessman and his wife once took a much-needed getaway at an oceanside hotel. During their stay a powerful storm arose, lashing the beach and sending massive breakers against the shore. The storm woke the man. He lay still in bed listening to the storm's fury and reflecting on his own life of constant and continual demands and pressures.

Before daybreak the wind subsided. The man got out of bed to go outside and survey the damage done by the storm. He walked along the beach and noticed it was covered with starfish that had been thrown ashore by the massive waves. They lay helpless on the sandy beach. Unable to get to the water, the starfish faced inevitable death as the sun's rays dried them out.

Farther down the beach, the man saw a figure walking along the shore. The figure kept stopping to stoop and pick something up. In the dim of the early-morning twilight, he couldn't quite make it all out. As he approached, he realized it was a young boy picking up the starfish one at a time and flinging them back into the ocean to safety.

As the man neared the young boy, he said, "Why are you doing that? One person will never make a difference—there are too many starfish to get back into the water before the sun comes up."

The boy said sadly, "Yes, that's true," and then bent to pick up another starfish. Then he said, "But I can sure make a difference to that one."

God never intended for an individual to solve all of life's problems. But He did intend for each one of us to use whatever resources and gifts He gave us to make a difference where we are.[10]

HE ONLY IS A WELL-MADE
MAN WHO HAS GOOD
DETERMINATION.

RALPH WALDO EMERSON

SERENDIPITY MOMENTS

*S*erendipity, according to Merriam-Webster's Collegiate Dictionary, is "the faculty or phenomenon of finding valuable or agreeable things not sought for." We sometimes call it an "accident, dumb luck, or fate," but serendipity has given us new products and better ways of doing things.

WE ARE HIS
WORKMANSHIP,
CREATED IN
CHRIST JESUS
UNTO GOOD
WORKS.

EPHESIANS 2:10 KJV

We all know examples of serendipity, such as Columbus's discovery of America while searching for a route to India. Maple syrup was discovered by Native Americans when, needing water, they tapped a maple tree and made the first maple syrup as they boiled off the sap. Westward-traveling pioneers looking for water stopped at a stream for a drink and found gold nuggets in the water.

While George Ballas was driving his car through a car wash, he had a moment of serendipity that made him a millionaire. As he watched the strings of the brushes cleaning his car, he turned his mind to his list of things to do, among them edging his lawn.

Suddenly an idea "popped" into his head. He took another long look at the strings on the rotating brush. The strings straightened out when turning at high speed, but they were still flexible enough to reach into every nook and cranny of his car to get it clean. He asked himself, *Why not use a nylon cord, whirling at high speed, to trim the grass and weeds around the trees and the house?* His idea—his serendipity—led to the invention of the Weedeater.

Where do we get new ideas? God is the Master behind serendipity! He may not always give you a million-dollar idea, but He will make you more creative. One expert gives this advice: Capture the ideas, jot them down quickly before they are gone, and evaluate them later. Take time to daydream with the Lord. Seek new challenges. Expand your perspective. Learn and do new things.[11]

Remember today that God is your Creator—and the Creator of everything in the universe. Ask Him to inspire you with new ideas that can glorify Him and benefit others. We are co-creators with Him!

SHOOT FOR THE MOON, AND
YOU MIGHT REACH A STAR.

VICTOR RAYFER

Open Door to
Your Goal

*E*dwin C. Barnes had a burning desire to become a business associate of the great inventor Thomas A. Edison. He didn't want to work *for* Edison, he wanted to work *with* him.

As a step toward making his dream come true, Barnes applied for a job at Edison's lab in New Jersey. He was hired as an office worker at a minimum salary—a far cry from a partnership. Months passed with no change in his status or his relationship with Edison. Most people would have given up, feeling their job was taking them nowhere. Barnes, however, stayed on board. He became thoroughly aware of the office environment and each person's job, and he sought out ways to make each person's work more pleasant and efficient. Above all, he remained open and optimistic. He saw all that he did as preparation for the day when he would become a partner with Edison in a joint venture.

THEREFORE, AS WE HAVE OPPORTUNITY, LET US DO GOOD TO ALL.

GALATIANS 6:10 NKJV

The day came when Edison presented the Edison Dictating Machine to his sales staff. They didn't believe it would sell. Barnes, however, saw this awkward-looking machine as his opportunity! He approached Edison, announcing he'd like to sell the dictating device. Since no one else had showed any enthusiasm for it, Edison gave him the chance. He granted him an exclusive contract to distribute and market the office machine throughout America. Barnes succeeded in his goal of working *with* the great inventor, and he achieved his goal to be a success in business at the same time.

Do you have a goal in your mind or heart today? You can be certain you will reach it as you serve others and help them reach their goals. The help you offer to a family member, neighbor, coworker, or employer today will come back to you in success tomorrow.

Opportunity may arrive in your life today in the disguise of misfortune, defeat, rejection, or failure. See beyond the problems to consider the possibilities. Step out to help someone overcome their difficulties, and you will be overwhelmed by the good fortune God sends your way!

SELF-CONFIDENCE IS THE FIRST
REQUISITE TO GREAT UNDERTAKINGS.

SAMUEL JOHNSON

PAYOFFS

THE MEN DID THE WORK FAITHFULLY.

2 CHRONICLES 34:12 RSV

*T*homas Edison once said:

> I am wondering what would have happened to me if some fluent talker had converted me to the theory of the eight-hour day, and convinced me that it was not fair to my fellow workers to put forth my best efforts in my work. I am glad that the eight-hour day had not been invented when I was a young man. If my life had been made up of eight-hour days, I do not believe I could have accomplished a great deal. This country would not amount to as much as it does if the young men had been afraid that they might earn more than they were paid.

Edison attributed his success to "1 percent inspiration and 99 percent perspiration."

Missionary and explorer David Livingstone worked rush-hour days in a factory—from 6:00 A.M. to 8:00 P.M. When he got off work, he attended night school classes for two hours, and then he went home to study late into the night.

Leonardo da Vinci, the great fifteenth-century Italian painter, sculptor, architect, engineer, and scientist, also understood the need for hard work. He said, "Thou, O God, doth sell to us all good things at the price of labor. Work is the seed from which grows all good things you hope for."

Nature also provides a striking example of hard work. Honey bees collect nectar from 125 clover heads to make one gram of honey. That adds up to three million trips to make one pound of honey!

And Michelangelo, one of the greatest artists of all time, disputed the marvel of his own talent. "If people knew how hard I have had to work to gain my mastery, it wouldn't seem wonderful at all."

"Overnight" success, making it big, and "lucking out" often disguise hard work.

Thank God every morning that you have something to do which must be done, whether you like it or not. Then do it to the best of your ability.

NEVER TURN DOWN A JOB
BECAUSE YOU THINK IT'S
TOO SMALL, YOU DON'T
KNOW WHERE IT CAN LEAD.

JULIA MORGAN

RUNNING PERSISTENTLY

*B*ob Kempainen was determined to make the 1996 United States Men's Olympic marathon team. He was willing to go to any lengths, no matter how gut-wrenching.

On a hilly course in Charlotte, North Carolina, he won the trials—but was sick five times in the last two miles.

Kempainen, the American record-holder in the marathon, has experienced stomach troubles since junior high school. But that hasn't kept this medical student from pursuing marathoning.

"To stop was out of the question," he said, when asked about his physical condition. With the goal in sight, he knew there would be plenty of time to rest after the race, during the five months that it would take to prepare for Atlanta.

When God puts a desire in your heart to achieve a specific goal, you can have the confidence that He will give you the strength and the ability to accomplish it.

IT IS GOD WHO ARMS ME WITH STRENGTH AND MAKES MY WAY PERFECT. HE MAKES MY FEET LIKE THE FEET OF A DEER; HE ENABLES ME TO STAND ON THE HEIGHTS.

2 SAMUEL 22:33-34

Every person has his or her own obstacles to overcome in life. In Kempainen's case, the condition of his stomach was trying to hinder him from winning the marathon race at the Olympics. In your life it will be something else. But we all face difficulties and challenges on the road to success—and the difference between those who succeed and those who fail is simply persistence.

Life is not a level, smooth path, but rather a series of hills and valleys. There are times spent on the mountaintop, when everything seems clear and perfect. Then there are those times when we feel like we're wandering around in a dark cavern, feeling our way along and trusting God for every step of faith.

Runners get a "second wind" after forcing themselves to go on when they feel like they can't. In the same way, we feel the joy of God's Spirit lift us up and carry us on when we choose to continue in faith, no matter how we feel or what's going on around us.

Take a moment and set your heart to be persistent in your faith—faith in God to lead you, pick you up when you have fallen, give you strength to go on, and ultimately bring you to victory.

THE RACE IS NOT ALWAYS TO THE SWIFT,
BUT TO THOSE WHO KEEP ON RUNNING.

UNKNOWN

What to Do

*A*n ancient Jewish story tells of a young traveler who encountered an old man at the edge of a forest. Staring into the darkness of the overgrown foliage in front of him, the young man asked his elder, "Can you tell me the best way through this forest?"

The wise old man replied, "I cannot."

IF ANY OF YOU LACKS WISDOM, LET HIM ASK OF GOD, WHO GIVES TO ALL MEN GENER-OUSLY AND WITHOUT REPROACH, AND IT WILL BE GIVEN TO HIM.

JAMES 1:5 NASB

The young man asked, "But haven't you lived here for a while? Surely you have been in the forest many times."

"Yes," the old man said, "and I can tell you all of the pitfalls and dangers I have encountered. I can tell you which paths *not* to take. But I have never been all the way through the forest. That is something you must experience for yourself."

Every day, we encounter all kinds of problems which others may have faced before us. It is a good thing to ask for advice in these matters. In truth, however, every set of problems has its own unique twists and turns. These subtle differences make each situation unique.

The best advice others give us may very well fall into the category of things "not to do." We can learn from the mistakes of others, and from our own, but in the end, the solution to *our* new and specific problem will be new and unique.

It is critical, therefore, for us to rely upon the counsel of the Lord every hour of the day and to ask specifically for His wisdom as we face questions, needs, or troubles. He knows the precise answer for the particular circumstance we face. He knows the beginning from the end!

Others may be experts at what *not* to do, or what is a *good* thing to do, but only the Lord can point us in the direction of what is *best* to do.

During this short break, ask the Lord to show you the *best* way to handle your day.

LIFE'S TRIALS MAY BE HARD TO BEAR,
BUT PATIENCE CAN OUTLIVE THEM.

MARTIN TUPPER

Use That
Powerful Engine!

IT IS GOD WHO ARMS ME WITH
STRENGTH AND MAKES MY WAY PERFECT.

PSALM 18:32

What a pleasure it is to drive a car with a powerful engine on a level highway! Picture a sunny day when there's no traffic and you're not in a hurry to get anywhere. You sing along with your favorite music tape and enjoy driving solely for driving's sake.

We are more likely to find ourselves in a much less powerful vehicle, however, while climbing a series of steep hills . . . in the rain . . . with lots of traffic behind us and in front of us . . . and late for an appointment.

But in our personal lives, is it possible to ride the rougher road and have the same peace and tranquillity inside as when we drive the level highway? The Bible says it is. God is our powerful Engine. He makes the difficult highway become manageable.

Perhaps your day started out smoothly, but by now you've left the easy stretch of road and come to the rolling hills. Now more than ever is the time to remind yourself that your Father in Heaven loves you and wants to help you.

With God's strength, you can stay alert and focused, maintaining an even pace and an even temperament regardless of the challenge. He will help you work through any problems that arise without compromising your integrity. He may even show you some shortcuts— and the gas mileage is great!

All you have to do is ask God to strengthen you and get you back on the road. Before you know it, you will be on the mountaintop with a clear view!

I'M NOT AFRAID OF STORMS,
FOR I'M LEARNING HOW
TO SAIL MY SHIP.

LOUISA MAY ALCOTT

THE SPICE OF LIFE

*M*ost of us have a routine we follow every morning. There's also a certain routine for our jobs, and another one that takes over after work. Even on the weekends, there are things that must be done.

BECAUSE OF THE LORD'S GREAT LOVE WE ARE NOT CONSUMED, FOR HIS COMPASSIONS NEVER FAIL. THEY ARE NEW EVERY MORNING; GREAT IS YOUR FAITHFULNESS.

LAMENTATIONS 3:22-23

Have you come to dread another sink full of dishes, another load of laundry, another car to wash, another lawn to mow, another rug to vacuum, or another floor to scrub? Is there any end to the "routine" of life?

There's no getting out of most of those chores. Someone has to keep things clean and running smoothly. But the one thing we *can* control is our attitude toward it all.

Rather than emphasizing the "same old," we should remember what the Bible says: "If anyone is in Christ, he is a new creation; the old has gone, the new has come!" (2 Corinthians 5:17) and, "I will

give you a new heart and put a new spirit in you"
(Ezekiel 36:26).

God never changes, but He loves variety. He wants
us to embrace life and keep our eyes open for new
possibilities, our minds open to new ideas, and our
hearts open to new people who cross our path.

Even in the midst of the "same old, same old" daily
routine, He can bring something new, unusual, and
different. Sometimes upsetting the routine can be
distressing. But don't let it shake your confidence in
God's plan for your life; instead, let it enhance His plan.

This morning, be aware that whether life seems to
have a "sameness" or has turned chaotic, you are
always changing inside. Through it all, the Lord is
continually stirring new life within you, giving you new
dreams and goals, and molding you to be more like
Jesus today!

NOTHING IS TO BE MORE HIGHLY PRICED
THAN THE VALUE OF EACH DAY.

WOLFGANG JOHANN VON GOETHE

THE STILL, SMALL VOICE

In his book *Focus on the Family,* Rolf Zettersten writes about his good friend Edwin who bought a new car. The car had lots of extra features—among them was a recording of a soft female voice, which gently reminded him if he had failed to fasten his seat belt or was running low on fuel. Appropriately, Edwin dubbed the voice "the little woman."

On one of his many road trips, "the little woman" began informing him that he needed to stop and fill his tank with gasoline. "Your fuel level is low," she cooed in her soft voice. Edwin nodded his head knowingly and thanked her with a smile. He decided, however, that he had enough gas to take him at least another fifty miles, so he kept on driving.

MY CONSCIENCE IS CLEAR, BUT THAT DOES NOT MAKE ME INNOCENT. IT IS THE LORD WHO JUDGES ME.

1 CORINTHIANS 4:4

The problem was, in only a few minutes the little lady spoke the warning again—and again and again and again until Edwin was ready to scream. Even though he knew, logically, that the recording was simply repeating itself, it really seemed as though the little woman spoke more and more insistently each time.

Finally he'd had all he could take. He pulled to the side of the road and, after a quick search under the dashboard for the appropriate wires, gave them a good yank. *So much for the little woman,* he thought.

He was still feeling very smug for having had the last say when his car began hissing and coughing. He had run out of gas! Somewhere inside the dashboard, he was almost certain he could hear the laughter of a woman!

Our Manufacturer, God, has given us a factory-installed warning voice. It's called the conscience. Sometimes we may think it's a nuisance, overly insistent, or just plain wrong. However, most of us will learn sooner or later that it is often trying to tell us exactly what we need to know.

Whether you are being told to stop for gas or being warned not to turn off the main road, your conscience knows what is right. Follow it today, and see if you don't experience more peace about every decision you make.

TEACH US TO PUT OUR TRUST IN THEE
AND TO AWAIT THY HELPING HAND.

TRADITIONAL AMISH PRAYER

THE RETURN ON GIVING

"GIVE, AND IT WILL BE GIVEN TO YOU:
GOOD MEASURE, PRESSED DOWN, SHAKEN
TOGETHER, AND RUNNING OVER."

LUKE 6:38 NKJV

A drowning man gestured frantically to a man standing at the edge of a swimming pool. Splashing his way until he was within arm's reach of the side of the pool, the drowning man hollered: "Here, let me give you my hand." The man reached down into the water, took the outstretched hand, and pulled the distressed man to safety. Afterward the lifesaver told the man he had rescued, "I find it unusual that you said 'Let me give you my hand,' rather than asking me to give you my hand."

The rescued man replied, "I work for a charitable organization, sir. I've discovered that people are always more willing to receive than they are to give!"

While the tendency of our human nature may be to receive more than to give, the Gospel tells us giving is actually the most productive way to receive! Whatever we extend to others, give to others, or do for others comes back to us multiplied. This principle has been recognized by the business community. Donald David has said:

> You never get promoted when no one else knows your current job. The best basis for being advanced is to organize yourself out of every job you're put in. Most people are advanced because they're pushed up from people underneath them rather than pulled by the top.

Find ways to give to those around you today. Especially to those who may be in subordinate positions. Freely share information with them, and be generous in your praise and encouragement. Give advice on how to do specific tasks more quickly, more efficiently, or with greater quality. You will find that the more you do to help others in their work, the easier your own workload will become.

MAKE YOURSELF NECESSARY
TO SOMEBODY.

RALPH WALDO EMERSON

ANOTHER POINT OF VIEW

On July 15, 1986, Roger Clemens, the sizzling right-hander for the Boston Red Sox, started his first All-Star Game. In the second inning he came to bat, something he hadn't done in years because of the American League's designated-hitter rule. He took a few uncertain practice swings and then looked out at his forbidding opponent, Dwight Gooden, who had won the Cy Young Award the previous year.

Gooden wound up and threw a white-hot fastball that flew right by Clemens. With an embarrassed smile on his face, Clemens stepped out of the box and asked catcher Gary Carter, "Is that what my pitches look like?"

"You bet it is!" replied Carter. Although Clemens quickly struck out, he went on to pitch three perfect innings and was named the game's most valuable player. With a fresh reminder of how overpowering a good fastball is, he later said from that day on he pitched with far greater boldness.

WE SAY WITH CONFIDENCE, "THE LORD IS MY HELPER; I WILL NOT BE AFRAID. WHAT CAN MAN DO TO ME?"

HEBREWS 13:6

Occasionally we forget the power we have at our disposal when it comes to speaking the Gospel of Jesus Christ. Maybe we need to step to the other side of the plate for a moment to be reminded!

The Holy Spirit within us always provides a powerful witness. We can "pitch" the Gospel with the confidence and authority that God has given us. But too many times, we weakly toss out a word here and there about Jesus, hoping not to make too great a stir. After all, we don't want to be too pushy, politically incorrect, or called a fanatic! We step up to the plate of opportunity without real conviction. Is it any wonder we seem to have no impact?

If you have an opportunity today, tell someone about how Jesus has changed your life with the conviction and power that comes from your heart. This is the power of the Holy Spirit within you. Then have peace in knowing you have done your part, and the rest is up to Him!

OPPORTUNITIES MULTIPLY AS THEY ARE
SEIZE; THEY DIE WHEN NEGLECTED.

UNKNOWN

COUNTING THE COST

*I*magine a natural disaster strikes your town and destroys everyone's home, as well as all the businesses, community services, recreation areas, and houses of worship. The government predicts that it will take nearly a decade to rebuild.

"WHICH OF YOU, INTENDING TO BUILD A TOWER, SITTETH NOT DOWN FIRST, AND COUNTETH THE COST, WHETHER HE HAVE SUFFI-CIENT TO FINISH IT?"

LUKE 14:28 KJV

That's what happened to Valmeyer, Illinois, during the Midwest floods of 1993. People who had been neighbors for most of their lives lost everything except their determination to stick together. So they decided to start over and rebuild together—in record time.

To accomplish such a monumental task, people had to step away from their normal lives and commit to new tasks. After all, there were buildings to construct, federal and state funds to secure, and utilities and social services to restore. An entire town had to be relocated and rebuilt from the ground up.

In this case, a little motivation went a long way. The $22 million project was completed by the end of 1996—barely three years after the flood. The statement by Helen Keller, "Every day we should do a little more than is required," could have been the motto of the people of Valmeyer. They took that sentiment to heart and rebuilt their town.[12]

Is there something in your life that you could accomplish much sooner by "counting the cost" and then doing a little extra every day, every week, or every month? Financial advisers tell us that home mortgages can be paid off years in advance by adding only $100 a month to the principal payment. Faster weight loss can be achieved by cutting out just 100 extra calories a day. Every project seems to have a momentum that is accelerated when we do "just a little more."

Focus on something that is important to you, and then map out a strategy for an "extra" touch.

GOING THE EXTRA MILE
BEGINS WITH A FOOT.

UNKNOWN

TURNING DARKNESS INTO LIGHT

> YOU, O LORD, KEEP MY LAMP
> BURNING; MY GOD TURNS
> MY DARKNESS INTO LIGHT.
>
> PSALM 18:28

It shouldn't take a serious illness to make us stop running around and discover what's really important, but sometimes it does. Sometimes a catastrophe can be a blessing in disguise.

Roger Bone, a physician in Ohio, was diagnosed with renal cancer. Surgeons recommended his right kidney and adrenal gland be removed. After the diagnosis, some of us might have isolated ourselves, become bitter and afraid, or tried to deny that anything serious was wrong. Roger Bone teaches us there's a better approach. He says these four observations have become "a way of life" for him:

1. Good health is often taken for granted; however, it is the most precious commodity one possesses.

2. One's spouse, children, family, and friends are the essential ingredients that allow one to endure an experience such as a serious illness.

3. When faced with death, one realizes the importance of God and one's relationship to God.

4. The things one does throughout life that seem so urgent are, most of the time, not so important.[13]

You can come through the fires of your life with the same positive outlook. Begin today by considering what you value most and hold dearest in life. You may be surprised how your priorities change—and how much richer your life becomes.

REFLECT UPON YOUR
PRESENT BLESSINGS, OF
WHICH EVERYONE HAS MANY.

CHARLES DICKENS

Making It to the Top

After breaking your back and your ribs, it's very important to regroup. Just ask Jaroslav Rudy, a Czechoslovakian man who has been living in the United States for the past few years.

One day he was riding his motorcycle on a remote trail. While taking a corner a little too fast, he hit a rock and lost control of his bike. Seconds later, he found himself at the bottom of a thirty-foot embankment—out of view to anyone who might be riding or walking on the trail.

For two days, Rudy stayed where he'd landed, too injured to move. Freezing temperatures, hunger, and pain finally drove him to try to get back to the trail.

His first attempts were futile—the pain was simply too intense. The next day, beginning at 6 A.M., he tried again. Crawling inch by inch for six hours, listening to the sounds of his injured bones crunching, and losing consciousness several times, he finally reached the trail. That's where four bicyclists spotted him.

A short time later, he was on his way to a hospital.

When your strength is gone and there's a goal you simply must achieve, you don't have to give up, but you do have to be sensible.

- Examine your situation, taking the time to analyze what needs to be done and what resources you have available. Ask the Lord to give you His wisdom and plan.
- Devise a plan of attack, including a timetable for what you hope to accomplish in any given period.
- Take short breaks along the way—to allow your creativity and energy to be renewed.
- Always remember that no matter how much success you achieve, you never really do it alone.

LET US THEN BE UP AND DOING, WITH A HEART FOR ANY FATE; STILL ACHIEVING, STILL PURSUING, LEARN TO LABOR AND TO WAIT.

H. W. LONGFELLOW

OPEN THE DOOR!

A rabbi was visited by a number of learned men one day. He surprised them by asking them this question: "Where is the dwelling of God?"

The men laughed at him, saying, "What a thing to ask! Is not the whole world full of His glory?"

The rabbi answered his own question. "God dwells wherever people let Him in."

We look at the abundance of problems of our world and become overwhelmed by the hunger, disease, abuse, crime, and so forth. Some of us point to Heaven and say, "Where is God? Why doesn't He do something?"

In truth, the Lord is looking at these same situations and crying, "Where are My people? Why don't they do something?"

Perhaps the foremost thing we can do to tackle the problems of our age is this: invite God into our lives.

When we invite the Lord into our daily lives, we experience His peace, and we have a growing understanding of how to live according to His plan. His indwelling Holy Spirit transforms us into people who manifest love, care, and morality.

Walking with the Lord every day in this way will cause productivity to flow in your life. He will tell you what problems you are to tackle and how. He will bring people to help you accomplish what He's asked you to do.

Invite God into every place you go today—the shop, factory, business, or school. Ask Him to be a part of every encounter and relationship. He has promised to "come in" to every door that is opened to Him!

WHEN WE WALK WITH THE LORD, IN
THE LIGHT OF HIS WORD, WHAT A
GLORY HE SHEDS ON OUR WAY!

HYMN: "TRUST AND OBEY"—J. H. SAMMIS

Fresh Breezes

We live our daily lives at such a fast pace, we often don't get beyond the most superficial level. We skim through magazines and books. We channel surf the programs on television. We purchase food in a drive-through and eat it on the way to our next destination. We listen to "sound bites" of opinions on the nightly news and leave thirty-second phone messages on answering machines. We condense research and opinions into "memo" form.

James Carroll addressed this tendency, writing:

We spend most of our time and energy in a kind of horizontal thinking. We move along the surface of things going from one quick base to another, often with a frenzy that wears us out. We collect data, things, people, ideas, "profound experiences," never penetrating any of them. . . . But there are other times. There are times when we stop. We sit still. We lose ourselves in a pile of leaves or its memory. We listen and breezes from a whole other world begin to whisper.[14]

Perhaps the best thing you can do during your coffee break today is nothing! Shut yourself off from your colleagues. Turn off the ringer on the phone. Stare out the window, and put your mind and heart into neutral.

Communication with God—prayer—is a two-way conversation! It is not just the voicing of praise and petitions, but it is also communion, sitting in silence with God, listening for whatever He may want to say. Simply enjoy the fact that He is, and you are, and you have a relationship with Him. These special moments with God are when His fresh breezes can enter your heart and refresh you.

THE ART OF SILENCE IS AS GREAT AS THAT OF SPEECH.

GERMAN PROVERB

STAY IN THE GAME

*Y*ou don't have to be a chess player to appreciate what happened in Philadelphia on February 17, 1996. Man defeated computer in an internationally-observed classical chess match.

Garry Kasparov, world chess champ, didn't win quite so easily as he had hoped to. He lost the first of the six games to Deep Blue, the IBM supercomputer. It was just what he needed, however, because it forced him to pay even closer attention, devise more intricate strategies, and learn more about a sport in which he is an acknowledged expert.

Kasparov notched three wins of his own and two draws in the remaining five games of the week-long match. It took every bit of chess knowledge he possessed—and some he developed along the way — to defeat a computer that is capable of calculating fifty billion positions in just three minutes.

When you have to face a "challenger" who seems to outweigh you, what can you do?

1. Have confidence in your own abilities, but don't get cocky.
2. If possible, prepare beforehand. That means study and practice.
3. Do a test run, with simulated "game" conditions (for example, give the speech or read the report in front of a family audience).
4. During your warm-ups, take short breaks. Use them to evaluate how you're doing or just to give your mind a rest.
5. Pray!

On "game day," relax. Let all the information you've stored in your brain rise to the top. Expect the unexpected, and be ready to improvise and make midcourse adjustments as needed. And, save a little something for the next game!

HIDE NOT YOUR TALENTS, THEY
FOR USE WERE MADE. WHAT'S
A SUN-DIAL IN THE SHADE?

BENJAMIN FRANKLIN

STAY INVOLVED

*Y*ou know it's a bad day when . . . your twin sister forgets your birthday. Your income tax refund check bounces. You put both contact lenses in the same eye. You wake up in traction in the hospital, and your insurance agent says your accident policy covers falling off the roof, but not hitting the ground.

How do we recover from those times when everything seems to go wrong? How do we cope when things seem to go from bad to worse?

The temptation during those times is to focus on ourselves and on the problems that seem to be relentless. But the best thing to do is just the opposite—get involved with other people.

Comedian George Burns said the key to happiness is helping others:

TRUST IN THE
LORD, AND
DO GOOD.

PSALM 37:3 KJV

If you were to go around asking people what would make them happier, you'd get answers like a new car, a bigger house, a raise in pay, winning a lottery, a face-lift, more kids, less kids, a new restaurant to go to—probably not one in a hundred would say a chance to help people. And yet that may bring the most happiness of all.

I don't know Dr. Jonas Salk, but after what he's done for us with his polio vaccine, if he isn't happy, he should have that brilliant head of his examined. Of course, not all of us can do what he did. I know I can't do what he did; he beat me to it.

But the point is, it doesn't have to be anything that extraordinary. It can be working for a worthy cause, performing a needed service, or just doing something that helps another person.[15]

What are some ways to help others? Smile or lend a helping hand to a stressed coworker. Write thank-you notes or cards to let distant friends know you are thinking of them. Be imaginative and creative in your deeds of kindness. On those bad days when nothing seems to go right . . . *you* can contribute something "right!"

TO PRESERVE A FRIEND THREE THINGS ARE NECESSARY: TO HONOR HIM PRESENT, PRAISE HIM ABSENT, AND ASSIST IN HIS NECESSITIES.

ITALIAN PROVERB

WHAT NATURE?

THE LORD IS MY SHEPHERD [TO FEED,
GUIDE, AND SHIELD ME], I SHALL
NOT LACK. . . . ONLY GOODNESS,
MERCY, AND UNFAILING LOVE SHALL
FOLLOW ME ALL THE DAYS OF MY LIFE.

PSALMS 23:1,6 AMP

How do you picture God? Many people see Him as a stern Judge, just waiting to pounce on those who break His laws. Others see Him as the Supreme Power of the universe, distant and remote, uninvolved in their lives. Still others have come to enjoy a loving, intimate relationship with their Heavenly Father.

Danish theologian Sören Kierkegaard provides a wonderful word picture in this prayer:

Father in Heaven, when the thought of Thee wakes in our hearts, let it not awaken like a frightened bird that flies about in dismay, but like a child waking from its sleep with a heavenly smile.

How we regard God has a direct impact on how we pray, as well as how we treat others. If we see God as a stern Judge, we tend to be more judgmental and less forgiving, even to ourselves. Our prayers, if we are brave enough to pray them, tend to be focused on requests for forgiveness and petitions for retribution on our enemies.

If we see God as distant and remote, we are likely to dismiss Him from our lives completely, turning to others for love and acceptance. Ultimately, we become frustrated because no one can give us the unconditional love that God can.

However, if we believe in God as our loving, generous Heavenly Father, we are much more likely to communicate with Him about *everything*. We are also more willing to communicate with others and forgive them for their frailties and faults.

In the end, every aspect of our lives, including work, is impacted by the nature of our relationship with God.

How do *you* regard Him?

GOD LOVES EACH OF
US AS IF THERE WERE
ONLY ONE OF US.

UNKNOWN

WHO'S WATCHING?

Even though we are Christians, we have to live our lives and conduct our businesses like everyone else, right? After all, we are only human!

Wrong! Once we have accepted Jesus into our lives, we have the supernatural power of the Holy Spirit to help us be and do more than what is humanly possible. Even nonbelievers know that people who call themselves followers of Christ should operate differently than those who don't.

> WALK WORTHY OF GOD, WHO HATH CALLED YOU UNTO HIS KINGDOM AND GLORY.
>
> 1 THESSALONIANS 2:12 KJV

Take, for instance, this account of a man named Roy. He had been a kidnapper and holdup man for twelve years, but while in prison he heard the Gospel and invited Jesus Christ into his life. He recalls: "Jesus said to me, 'I will come and live in you and we will serve this sentence together.' And we did."

Several years later he was paroled, and just before he went out, he was handed a two-page letter written by another prisoner, which read:

You know perfectly well that when I came into the jail I despised preachers, the Bible, and anything that smacked of Christianity. I went to the Bible class and the preaching service because there wasn't anything else interesting to do.

Then they told me you were saved, and I said, "There's another fellow taking the Gospel road to get parole." But, Roy, I've been watching you for two-and-a-half years. You didn't know it, but I watched you when you were in the yard exercising, when you were working in the shop, when you played, while we were all together at meals, on the way to our cells, and all over, and now I'm a Christian, too, because I watched you. The Savior who saved you has saved me. You never made a slip.

Roy says, "When I got that letter and read it, through, I broke out in a cold sweat. Think of what it would have meant if I had slipped, even once."[16]

Who might be secretly watching you? A coworker, a child, a boss, or a spouse who needs to know Jesus? Remember, you are His representative to that person.

OUR DEEDS DETERMINE US, AS MUCH
AS WE DETERMINE OUR DEEDS.

GEORGE ELIOT

On Call

*P*orch swings, picnic tables, and handwritten letters almost seem like relics of a bygone age. Symbols of today's fast-paced culture are fast-food drive-thrus, computer games, and e-mail. In spite of the changes in our cultural icons, we actually may not be that much busier than the last generation—after all, we still only have twenty-four hours in a day.

The problem is, however, that we seldom "get away from it all." Experts say that communication technology gives immediate access to anyone, virtually anywhere. We are no more than a beeper or a cellular phone-call away from being summoned.

O THAT I HAD WINGS LIKE A DOVE! I WOULD FLY AWAY AND BE AT REST.

PSALM 55:6 RSV

Because of that phenomenon, Dr. Mark Moskowitz of Boston University's Medical Center observes, "A lot of people are working twenty-four hours a day, seven days a week, even when they're not technically at work." That is a precursor to first-class exhaustion.

Government executive Roy Neel quit his job as deputy chief of staff in the Clinton Administration and took a slower-paced job. He realized that work "even for the President of the United States" was not worth the price. It hit home for Roy the night he and his nine-year-old son, Walter, were ready to walk out the door for a long-promised baseball game. The phone rang, and it was the president.

Walter was not impressed with a call from the White House. What he wanted was to go to a baseball game with his dad. After the hour-long phone call, Roy discovered his son had found a ride to the game with a neighbor. He commented, "Our society has become schizophrenic. We praise people who want balance in their lives, but reward those who work themselves to death."[17]

When asked his formula for success, physicist Albert Einstein spelled it out this way: "If A is success in life, then A equals X plus Y plus Z. Work is X, Y is play, and Z is keeping your mouth shut." What a genius!

> WORK, ALTERNATED WITH
> NEEDFUL REST, IS THE SALVATION
> OF MAN OR WOMAN.
>
> ANTOINETTE BROWN BLACKWELL

Good, Better, Best

I HAVE SET BEFORE YOU LIFE AND
DEATH, BLESSINGS AND CURSES.
NOW CHOOSE LIFE, SO THAT YOU AND
YOUR CHILDREN MAY LIVE AND THAT
YOU MAY LOVE THE LORD YOUR GOD,
LISTEN TO HIS VOICE, AND HOLD FAST
TO HIM. FOR THE LORD IS YOUR LIFE.

DEUTERONOMY 30:19-20

As children, we can't wait to grow up and finish school. In our twenties, we scramble for a job and try to decide which career is the best fit. In our thirties, we struggle to balance home and work.

In our forties, some of us face the empty nest and use the time to rediscover old passions or find new activities to challenge us. In our fifties, we make a last push to prepare for inevitable retirement. Movement, movement, movement.

Then, one day, the daily grind comes to an abrupt halt, and we have a choice to make: vegetate or keep moving.

If we're fortunate like Richard Wesley Hamming, we don't have to wonder how we'll fill the time. In the late 1940s, Hamming wrote the codes known as the Hamming Codes. They enable computers to correct their own mistakes. For the last twenty years he has been "educating admirals" in computer science at a Navy school.

Hamming, now eighty-one, admits the older he gets, the harder it is to stay enthused—but he's not quitting, and neither should you!

We can't always depend on others to inspire us, so how do we maintain our zest for living? Ask yourself this: *Will it be difficult to stay inspired in Heaven?* Not a chance! We will have perfect health and unlimited energy, and we will be in an environment of peace, love, and joy. The good news is, Jesus told us we don't have to wait for the kingdom of Heaven; it's inside of us. (See Luke 17:20-21.)

Today, when things get tough, look within and bring some Heaven to earth!

LAUNCH YOURSELF ON
EVERY WAVE FIND YOUR
ETERNITY IN EACH MOMENT.

HENRY DAVID THOREAU

MAKING A LIFE

*N*o doubt we would all agree with the sentiment "There's more to life than things." Yet much of our lives seem to be spent in the acquisition, maintenance, and disposal of material goods. Certainly we cannot enjoy the basics of food, shelter, and clothing without a concern for things.

BE CONSTANTLY RENEWED IN THE SPIRIT OF YOUR MIND [HAVING A FRESH MENTAL AND SPIRITUAL ATTITUDE].

EPHESIANS
4:23 AMP

The truly important things of life, however, are those which cannot be encountered by the physical senses, purchased with money, or placed on a shelf. When we take a look at what we value most in life we generally find family, friends, health, peace, contentment, laughter, helping others, and communion with the Lord foremost on our list of priorities.

One of the ways to get at the "free" things in life is to follow this advice of Sidney Lovett:

Give the best you have received from the past to the best that you may come to know in the future.

Accept life daily not as a cup to be drained but as a chalice to be filled with whatsoever things are honest, pure, lovely, and of good report. Making a living is best undertaken as part of the more important business of making a life.

Every now and again take a good look at something not made with hands—a mountain, a star, the turn of a stream. There will come to you wisdom and patience and solace, and above all, the assurance that you are not alone in the world.[18]

Meditate on the "intangibles" as you spend this time alone with the Lord. Take a moment to stare out a window or sit in a garden, and undertake the important business of making a life!

IT IS A GOOD THING TO BE RICH,
AND A GOOD THIING TO BE STRONG,
BUT IT IS A BETTER THING TO BE
LOVED BY MANY FRIENDS.

EURIPIDES

NOT WORTH A DIME

The story is told of a young man who was invited to preach at a church in Nashville, Tennessee. On an impulse he used as his text, "Thou shalt not steal."

The next morning he stepped onto a city bus and handed the driver a dollar bill. The driver handed him his change, and he walked to the rear of the bus to stand, since there were no seats available.

"THERE IS NOTHING CONCEALED THAT WILL NOT BE DISCLOSED, OR HIDDEN THAT WILL NOT BE MADE KNOWN."

LUKE 12:2

Once he had steadied himself, he counted his change. There was a dime too much. His first thought was, *The bus company will never miss this dime.*

By now the bus had stopped again, and the narrow aisle between him and the driver was one long line of people. Then it hit him, he could not keep money that did not belong to him.

After saying, "Excuse me" many times and receiving several scowling looks, he finally made his way to the front and said to the driver, "You gave me too much change."

The driver replied, "Yes, a dime too much. I gave it to you on purpose. You see, I heard your sermon yesterday, and I watched in my mirror as you counted your change. Had you kept the dime I would never again have had any confidence in preaching."

Imagine the outcome if this young man had decided the displeasure of his fellow passengers wasn't worth a dime's worth of honesty!

Our influence is like a shadow; it may fall even where we think we've never been. We also need to realize there are no "time-outs" or "vacations" we can take in keeping the Lord's commandments or being true to our conscience.

Stay on track with what you know is right!

HONEST MEN FEAR NEITHER
THE LIGHT NOR THE DARK.

THOMAS FULLER

SIGNPOSTS

*O*ne very dark night a man drove along a deserted road on his way to a place he had visited only once before. As he drove, he suddenly became uneasy, thinking he might have missed a turn two or three miles back.

He drove on mile after mile. Several times he slowed down, overcome by indecision. Should he turn around and drive back to that intersection, now ten miles behind him? If he was wrong, turning back would cost him an additional twenty or thirty minutes, and he was barely on schedule as it was.

Slower and slower he went. The tension built in his body as his hands gripped the steering wheel, and a knot of stress between his shoulders began to throb. He began to think, *Even if it's a mistake, I have to go back to reassure myself.*

Just as he was about to turn around, his headlights reflected off a white marker in the distance. He increased his speed and soon saw the familiar shield that marks United States highways. The number 82 was clearly visible, and that was the road he needed to take. He continued on his way with confidence.

Sometimes in the dark nights of our travel through life, we feel we've missed a turn or read a sign incorrectly. Knowing our indecision, God often gives us reassuring signs to help us re-establish our confidence in where we are heading.

If you find yourself confused and directionless today, God has placed bright signposts in your path—the cross and empty tomb of Jesus Christ. In them you can see the greatest markers of His love, and you can continue on the path He sets before you with full confidence.

NO MATTER HOW FAR YOU WANDER, YOUR HEART ALWAYS KNOWS THE WAY HOME.

CHERIE RAYBURN

Rise Gently and Slowly

Scuba diving is a sport that grows more and more popular every year. But those who take it up must be aware of the dangers it poses.

One of the biggest threats is decompression illness, or "the bends." While divers are under water, they breathe compressed air; its pressure is equal to that of the water around them. If divers stay down a long time and dive deeply, their bodies absorb a great deal of compressed gas. If they then ascend too quickly, their bodies can't expel the extra gases slowly enough to avoid the formation of bubbles in their body tissues.

TEACH US TO NUMBER OUR DAYS, THAT WE MAY PRESENT TO THEE A HEART OF WISDOM.

PSALM 90:12 NASB

When bubbles form in the brain, spinal cord, or nerves outside the central nervous system, the results can be paralysis, convulsions, lack of coordination, numbness, nausea, speech defects, and personality changes.

Divers suffering from decompression must be recompressed in a hyperbaric chamber and then gradually decompressed while breathing pure oxygen.

How can decompression be avoided? By ascending more slowly, with several interruptions along the way. Another method is taking a "safety stop" for several minutes at a depth of five or six meters.[19]

When it comes to our career, how quickly do we want to rise to the top? Is it worth getting "the bends" to arrive there faster than anyone else?

Each time you dive into your work at the beginning of the day, remember to gradually let go of it at the end of the day. Learn to wean yourself from it so you can relax and recuperate in the company of family or friends. Then you will get a good night's sleep before strapping on the tank bright and early the next morning.

GOD GIVE ME WORK TILL MY LIFE SHALL
END AND LIFE TILL MY WORK IS DONE.

WINEFRED HOLTBY

SMALL THINGS

In a certain bank there was a trust department in which four young men and one older man were employed. The directors decided to promote the older employee and then give one of the younger men his place as head of the department.

After considering the merits of each young man, the directors selected one of them for the new position and gave him a substantial increase in salary. They decided to notify him of the promotion that afternoon at four o'clock.

During the noon hour, the young man went to a cafeteria for lunch. One of the directors was behind him in line, with several other customers between them. The director saw the young man select his food, including a piece of butter. He proceeded to hide the butter under other food and lied to the cashier about what was on his plate.

"HE THAT IS FAITHFUL IN THAT WHICH IS LEAST IS FAITHFUL ALSO IN MUCH: AND HE THAT IS UNJUST IN THE LEAST IS UNJUST ALSO IN MUCH."

LUKE 16:10 KJV

That afternoon the directors notified the young man that they had intended to give him a promotion, but because of what had been seen in the cafeteria, they would have to discharge him instead. They could not have someone who would lie and steal as an employee of their bank.

What businesses call "employee theft" is often thought of by the employee as "borrowing." So open and prevalent are such "loans" that even committed Christians can fail to realize that what they are doing is stealing. And a few sheets of paper, pencils, long distance phone calls, Xerox copies, and extra time at lunch add up.

The next time you are tempted to "borrow" something from your employer, picture Jesus asking you where you got it!

SHALL WEALTH BE ALL OF WORLDLY THINGS, AND RICHNESS GAINED THROUGH GATHERED WARES? OR RATHER FOUND IN SILENT DAWNS, THE REVERENCE OF EVENING PRAYERS.

A. S. LEIGH

SOWING PEACE

> ## "BLESSED ARE THE PEACEMAKERS, FOR THEY SHALL BE CALLED SONS OF GOD."
>
> ### MATTHEW 5:9 RSV

The entire European continent felt the blows of hatred delivered by the evil tyrant Adolf Hitler. Millions of people died as a result of his platform of hate; millions more were scarred for life.

Heinz was an eleven-year-old Jewish boy who lived with his family in the Bavarian village of Furth during the 1930s. When Hitler's band of thugs came tearing through the village, Heinz's father lost his job as a schoolteacher, recreational activities were forbidden, and Furth's streets became battlegrounds.

Neighborhoods were terrorized by the Nazi youth looking to make trouble. The young Heinz always kept alert to stay clear of them. When he saw them coming, he sought cover to get out of their way.

One day, Heinz couldn't avoid a face-to-face encounter with a Nazi bully. A brutal beating seemed inevitable, but Heinz walked away from the fray without a scratch. This time he used his persuasive abilities and language skills to convince his enemy that a fight was not necessary. This would not be the last time this young Jewish boy would use his peacemaking skill in Nazi-occupied Europe.

Eventually Heinz and his family escaped to safety in America, where Heinz would make his mark. He became known as a mediator and peacemaker among world leaders and nations. The young boy who grew up as Heinz anglicized his name when he came to America. We know him as Henry Kissinger.

Today put your talents to use as a peacemaker to work together with those of different opinions. When you sow seeds of peace, you are doing God's work on earth, and you will reap a harvest of goodness.

TO PLOUGH IS TO PRAY,

TO PLANT IS TO PROPHESY,

AND THE HARVEST

ANSWERS AND FULFILLS.

ROBERT GREEN INGERSOLL

THE FISHERMAN

A wealthy man spent his days fishing in the lake beside his mansion. Every day, on the same lake he saw a poor man who lived in a rickety shack. The poor man fished with a stick and some string, and he sat only an hour or so, rarely catching more than two fish, then went home.

The years passed, and frustrated from too much thinking, the rich man approached the poor: "Please excuse me, but we've seen each other fishing here for years, and I'm curious. You sit here every day catching only a few fish and then heading home. I couldn't help but wonder why you don't stay longer.

"You see, if you just stayed one or two hours more each day, you could sell your extra fish in town. You could get enough money for a better fishing rod, then catch more fish. You could eventually get a boat and a net. Then with even more fish, you could hire another man and another boat. Soon you would not even have to be on the boats all day; you could have a huge company earning a lot of money. Then, you could easily spend your days fishing alone, for only as long as you would like, doing what you want with no worries."

"But, sir, I don't understand," said the poor man, "that's what I do now."[20]

To be content with the life God has given us is to live the richest life of all.

IF I'M CONTENT WITH A LITTLE,
ENOUGH IS AS GOOD AS A FEAST.

ISAAC BICKERSTAFFE

THE IMPORTANCE
OF EVERYDAY TALK

The banquet hall is festively adorned with beautiful flowers and ribbons. Across the front of the room a large banner reads, "A Golden Congratulations for a Golden Couple." It is their fiftieth wedding anniversary, and family and friends have gathered from far and near to pay tribute to them. The four children each take a turn at describing their fondest memories and greatest lessons learned from their parents. Then the cake is cut, pictures are taken, and everyone enjoys visiting with one another.

LET YOUR CONVERSATION BE ALWAYS FULL OF GRACE.

COLOSSIANS 4:6

Too soon, the afternoon draws to a conclusion. Friends say good-bye; family members repack mementos in the cars; and everyone leaves. Later that evening, one of the grandchildren asks, "What's the secret, Grandma, to being happily married for fifty years?"

Without hesitation, her grandmother replies, "We were always able to talk about everything."

Recent research supports her conclusion. A study of couples happily married for more than twenty-five years found only one thing they all had in common—each couple "chitchatted" with each other daily. Perhaps since they already know how to converse with one another, they are more able to talk out their differences when tough times come. The same most likely holds true for our relationship with God. If we commune with Him regularly, then we will automatically turn to Him first when crisis comes.

Have you had a quiet time talking with God today?

WITH GOD ALL THINGS BEGIN, WITH GOD LET ALL THINGS COME TO REST.

AMISH BIBLE BOOKPLATE, 1845

GREAT BEGINNINGS

> I PRESS ON TOWARD THE GOAL TO WIN
> THE PRIZE FOR WHICH GOD HAS CALLED
> ME HEAVENWARD IN CHRIST JESUS.
>
> PHILIPPIANS 3:14

In his best-seller *The Seven Habits of Highly Effective People,* Stephen Covey entitles one of the seven habits as "Begin with the End in Mind." He uses an illustration of imagining yourself at your own funeral. If you close your eyes and imagine the people in attendance, the flowers, the music, and the minister delivering the eulogy, how would it go if your life were to end today?

How would you want it to be?

Through his illustration, Covey demonstrates that, in order to achieve a goal, we must have that goal in mind in everything we do along the way.

More importantly, everything we do today—whether in line with our long-range desires or not—

affects what we become for the rest of our lives. And what we become affects everyone whose lives we touch. What a ripple effect! There's an old Chinese proverb that says:

> If there is light in the soul,
> There will be beauty in the person.
> If there is beauty in the person,
> There will be harmony in the house.
> If there is harmony in the house,
> There will be order in the nation.
> If there is order in the nation,
> There will be peace in the world.

If you remember the 70s, you'll recognize the phrase, "Today is the first day of the rest of your life." Today is our opportunity to begin with the end in mind. If we begin with God's light in our souls, we can bring beauty, harmony, order, and peace—the Prince of Peace—to the world.

IN SEED TIME LEARN,

IN HARVEST TEACH, IN

WINTER ENJOY.

WILLIAM BLAKE

My Heart for You

There is a story told of the famous escape artist Harry Houdini that gives a glimpse into his heart.

Early in his career when he was still an unknown vaudeville act, he and his young wife were living from week to week with no reserves of food or money. One afternoon he ventured out to the marketplace to purchase groceries. Within a few minutes, he returned and sat at the kitchen table weeping uncontrollably.

Uncertain what had happened, but fearing the worst, his wife tried to console him and to find out what had occurred. Finally, controlling his sobs, Harry related to her that he had not been harmed nor assaulted. It seems that on his way to the market, he came across a young man who was crippled and begging for food. Harry immediately gave the man all that he had and then returned to the apartment.

AS GOD'S CHOSEN PEOPLE, HOLY AND DEARLY LOVED, CLOTHE YOURSELVES WITH COMPASSION, KINDNESS, HUMILITY, GENTLENESS AND PATIENCE.

COLOSSIANS 3:12

Why then was Harry crying? He had done a very noble thing. Perhaps he was upset because he was too impulsive and now he and his wife had nothing left for them. No, he was not crying for them. He was crying because he had no more to give.

Harry Houdini demonstrated the greatest gift of all that day. He exhibited empathy, and it is empathy that keeps our hearts fresh and new. Thousands of years ago Homer said it like this:

Yet, taught by time, my heart has learned to glow
For others' good, and melt at others' woe.

WHATEVER YOU DO, DO IT WITH ALL YOUR MIGHT.

MARCUS TULLIUS CICERO

THE MAGIC OF
INSTRUCTIONS

*A*ngrily the young man flung his wrench across the driveway and rolled away from the car. He had been trying for hours to change the brake pads on his wife's small foreign car. It didn't help matters that he was, at best, a "mediocre" mechanic. Finally, in exasperation he stormed into the house and informed his wife that something was seriously wrong with her car and he could not fix it.

"In fact," he shouted, "I don't know if anyone can fix it!"

PAY ATTENTION
AND LISTEN TO
THE SAYINGS OF
THE WISE.

PROVERBS 22:17

She quietly thanked him for his efforts and then moved to the telephone where she called her father, a master mechanic. After she explained the situation, she and her father ventured to the nearest library, where they found a manual for her car. They carefully made copies of the pages giving directions on how to change the brake pads. Next, they stopped at a foreign car auto parts store and purchased a small but vital tool necessary for this particular job. Finally, they proceeded home to her car, and within thirty minutes the repair job was complete.

What made the difference? Three things: First, she contacted her father, a master mechanic. The first instruction God gives us is to call upon Him. Second, they found the right set of instructions and carefully followed them. Sometimes, we insist on trying to do things without consulting our instruction book, the Bible. Finally, they secured the proper tool to do the job. God will always give us the right tool if we will go to Him, asking for wisdom.

Whether we are talking about brake pads or critical life decisions, it is simply amazing—almost magical— how well things work out when we follow instructions.

GOD GRANT US GREAT FORTUNE AND BLESSINGS AND LEAD US BY YOUR WAY.

AMISH HYMNAL BOOKPLATE, 1858

I CAN SEE CLEARLY NOW

> WE KNOW THAT, WHEN HE APPEARS,
> WE SHALL BE LIKE HIM, BECAUSE WE
> SHALL SEE HIM JUST AS HE IS.
>
> 1 JOHN 3:2 NASB

*B*etween Macon and Valdosta, Georgia, lies a stretch of Interstate 75, known for heavy fog that causes massive pileups of cars, vans, trucks, and campers. Several times each year horrible accidents happen as drivers enter the thick fog. Many can't even see the front of their own vehicles, much less beyond.

The result is a disaster waiting to happen—and often it does. Many people are injured, vehicles are destroyed, and motorists are delayed for hours. The costs to personal property and the city and state, as well as the increase in insurance rates are astronomical. But the worst tragedy is the loss of human life.

Drivers involved in these accidents will tell you the same story. They saw the fog but didn't think it was as thick as it turned out to be. They hoped to pass through it safely by turning their blinkers on and driving slowly. These drivers had no idea that many vehicles in front of them had already been forced to stop—often victims of whatever tragedy had occurred to a car or truck ahead of them.

In this life, we may see things through a fog of sin or circumstances. But the day will come when we can stand before Christ, when we will see Him clearly just as He is, in all His glory. Nothing will be able to cloud the true and living Christ from our vision when we go to Heaven.

The good news is that we don't have to wait. Today, right now, we can see Him clearly through His Word and in the lives of our Godly brothers and sisters.

GIVE THY BLESSING, WE PRAY THEE, TO OUR DAILY WORK, THAT WE MAY DO IT IN FAITH, AND HEARTILY.

THOMAS ARNOLD

THE FIRST VALENTINE

*M*ost people would be surprised to learn that Valentine's Day was not intended to celebrate romance with gifts of flowers and chocolate. It was a day to honor a different kind of love.

Valentine was a Christian priest near Rome in a period when Christians were punished for rejecting the Roman gods.

WE LOVE,
BECAUSE HE
FIRST LOVED US.

1 JOHN 4:19 NASB

During this persecution, legends say that Valentine assisted Christians in escaping from prison. He was discovered, arrested, and sent to trial, where he was asked if he believed in the Roman gods. He called their gods false. He continued to say that the only true God was He whom Jesus called "Father."

Valentine was imprisoned, but it did not stop him from continuing his ministry. Even the prison guards began to listen to his witness. One was the adoptive father of a blind girl, whom the priest befriended as she waited at the jail while her father worked.

When the Roman emperor heard of Valentine's persistent worship of his God, he ordered his execution. In the days before his death, Valentine offered to pray for the jailer's blind daughter, and her sight was miraculously restored when he died. As a result, the jailer's entire family—forty-six people—came to believe in the one God and were baptized.

Saint Valentine knew every step of the way that his activities would endanger his life. But he continued because he loved God and people. It was a love that deserves to be honored and modeled after every day of the year.

MANY MEN GO FISHING ALL OF THEIR
LIVES WITHOUT KNOWING THAT
IT IS NOT FISH THEY ARE AFTER.

HENRY DAVID THOREAU

SEEK AND FIND

The parents of a teen were struggling with constant calls from their child's school, the youth director at church, and even other parents in the same community, all complaining about the behavior of their fifteen-year-old. Distraught and discouraged, the parents rose early one morning and sought the Lord on behalf of their child. Although not in the habit of praying together or for their children prior to this, they found the Lord there for them on that morning and every morning after that. This morning prayer time became the one time they longed for all during the day.

I LOVE THEM THAT LOVE ME; AND THOSE THAT SEEK ME EARLY SHALL FIND ME.

PROVERBS 8:17 KJV

Not only was the habit of praying together started, but reading the Bible together as well. Each day the Lord had many new lessons to teach them. They were learning and growing as individuals and as a couple, and soon they noticed positive changes in their daughter's behavior as well. Eventually, what the parents had begun as a united effort—to cry out for help to the Lord on their daughter's behalf—was fast becoming a time when the whole family would get together for devotions and worship.

When their daughter saw the transformation in her mother and father, she decided to make some changes in her life too. Today she is a Godly young woman who loves the Lord with all her heart.

When we seek the Lord for a specific need, we find He is ready to meet us for all our needs.

GOD ALWAYS ANSWERS US
IN THE DEEPS, NEVER IN THE
SHALLOWS OF OUR SOUL.

AMY CARMICHAEL

LET THE RIVER FLOW

The Dead Sea, located between Israel and Jordan, is famous as the lowest point on the surface of the earth. It is also a lively tourist attraction for its healthful spas, where visitors bathe in the salty seawater and flock to purchase cosmetics made from Dead Sea mud.

Have you ever wondered why it is called the Dead Sea? Unlike most large lakes, it has no outlet. The Jordan River flows into the Dead Sea, but nothing flows out. Without sharing what it receives, it dies.

The same is true for people. When we receive gifts of talent, education, financial fortune, or other resources, we might think sharing those gifts with others leaves less for us. But when you don't give of yourself to others, a part of you dies.

As Dr. David Livingstone once commented:

People talk of the sacrifice I have made in spending so much of my life in Africa. Can that be called a sacrifice which is simply acknowledging a great debt we owe to our God, which we can never repay? Is that a sacrifice which brings its own reward in healthful activity, the consciousness of doing good, peace of mind, and a bright hope of a glorious destiny? It is emphatically no sacrifice. Rather it is a privilege. . . . Of this we ought not to talk, when we remember the great sacrifice which He made Who left His Father's throne on high to give Himself for us.

May the river of God's love flow through us to everyone we meet.

NEVER UNDERTAKE

ANYTHING FOR WHICH

YOU WOULDN'T HAVE

THE COURAGE TO ASK

THE BLESSINGS OF HEAVEN.

GEORGE CHRISTOPH LIGHTENBERB

A REASON TO RISE

When we camp deep in the woods, the first sense that attracts our attention each morning is smell. The aromatic whiffs of food cooked over an open flame are a wonderful treat to awakening senses. The savory aroma of bacon, sausage, and a fresh pot of coffee gently moves through the forest and rests overhead just long enough to rouse us from our sleep and produce a memory like no other. Years later we talk about that experience as if we were reliving it, almost capable of smelling the coffee right then. It's a wake-up call campers fondly cherish.

ARISE, SHINE; FOR YOUR LIGHT HAS COME, AND THE GLORY OF THE LORD HAS RISEN UPON YOU.

ISAIAH 60:1 NASB

We all have moments like these that provide a platform for memories past that are special to us. These classic times of pleasure linger in our minds, much like the smells of a delicious breakfast on a long ago camping trip. The first call of the morning brings us into the new day and helps to set the pace and tone for the tasks ahead.

Could it be that as followers of Christ, we experience wake-up calls in our lives that are for more than just reminiscing? God can turn our wake-up calls, lessons learned, and "deserts crossed" into opportunities that allow His loving plans for our lives to shine through us to a lost and depraved world.

Isaiah shouted, "Arise, shine!" Share the joy of knowing Christ with others. There are many who would otherwise never awaken to become a child of God unless you share the joy of knowing Christ with them. Become the aroma of Christ.

A BIT OF FRAGRANCE ALWAYS CLINGS
TO THE HAND THAT GIVES YOU ROSES.

CHINESE PROVERB

MOMENT OF TRUTH

$\mathcal{W}$ith these words, Jean Shepherd introduces a delightful and poignant essay dealing with the trials of adolescence, specifically blind dates:

> There are about four times in a man's life, or a woman's, too, for that matter, when unexpectedly, from out of the darkness, the blazing carbon lamp, the cosmic searchlight of Truth shines full upon them. It is how we react to those moments that forever seals our fate.[21]

In the story, a fourteen-year-old boy agrees, against his better judgment, to go on a blind date.

TEACH ME THY WAY, O LORD; I WILL WALK IN THY TRUTH.

PSALM 86:11 KJV

The gist of the tale is that, contrary to all the logic of blind dates, his date, Junie Jo Prewitt, is beautiful. In fact, she "made Cleopatra look like a Girl Scout." As the evening progresses however, he becomes aware that Junie Jo is *not* enjoying the date, and in a moment of truth he realizes, "I am the blind date."[22] This is an extremely painful moment of truth when he faces that fact that where he was worried that his *date* might not be someone he would want to be with, the truth is that *he* is someone Junie Jo does not want to be seen with.

Shepherd concludes the story with the line: "I didn't say much the rest of the night. There wasn't much to be said."[23]

Life usually presents us with moments of truth—times when we have no choice but to see ourselves just as we really are. And, as Shepherd says, "It is how we react in those moments that really matters."

Moments of truth come each day. When these moments do come, we need to seek guidance and act with humility; for we are only as spiritual as our last decision.

LIFE IS SHORT, BUT THERE IS ALWAYS TIME FOR COURTESY.

RALPH WALDO EMERSON

Shining Light

"LET YOUR LIGHT SHINE BEFORE MEN
IN SUCH A WAY THAT THEY MAY SEE
YOUR GOOD WORKS, AND GLORIFY
YOUR FATHER WHO IS IN HEAVEN."

MATTHEW 5:16 NASB

*U*pon waking in the morning, most of us have regular duties we follow or some established routine to make ourselves presentable for the day. Many of us would never allow certain friends or relatives to see us when we first crawl out of bed. Most of us would rather die than to have the "real us" exposed before we have showered, shaved, made up our faces and hair, and brushed our teeth.

Although there is nothing wrong with wanting to present ourselves looking our best, there needs to also be something on the inside that radiates who Christ is in us.

When a piece of coal is placed on top of a sizzling hot bed of ashes, it soon catches the flame and begins to burn in brilliant colors as it radiates heat for long periods of time. However, if we took that same piece of coal away from the flame, it would quickly lose its glow and burn out. The brilliance would disappear, and the heat from it would rapidly diminish. Nothing would be left except a big, black, useless lump.

We become useless without a fresh daily infusion of His power and grace. Beginning the day in the presence of the Lord guarantees that His light will shine through us before others with a brilliance. Sitting at His feet and allowing Him to be our Teacher before the day begins provides us with the spark that exposes areas of our lives in which the Lord needs to do His cleansing or healing work.

THE MORE WE DEPEND
ON GOD, THE MORE
DEPENDABLE WE FIND HE IS.

CLIFF RICHARDS

WHAT OF WALLS?

The following lines from poet Robert Frost's famous work "Mending Wall" hit right at the heart of the challenge of maintaining proper relationships:

> I let my neighbor know beyond the hill;
> > And on a day we meet to walk the line
> > And set the wall between us once again.[24]

The poem both celebrates tradition and pokes fun at it at the same time. Many individuals over the years have debated its most famous line: "Good fences make good neighbors."

Frost himself takes issue with the need for carefully maintained boundaries when he attempts to get a rise out of his neighbor by asking, "Why do they make good neighbors?"

Getting no response, he goes on to say, "Something there is that doesn't love a wall, that wants it down."

Still no response, and in the closing lines he likens his neighbor to "an old stone savage armed, who will not go behind his father's saying."

Why do we seem to always be building walls between others and ourselves or between God and ourselves? Is it perhaps because we fear becoming vulnerable to rejection? Or do we simply feel an irresistible need to stake our claim to what we want as our own? In either case, it takes much courage to maintain proper respect for one another without building walls that separate us inappropriately.

Robert Frost urges us to be careful to know what we might be "walling in or out and to whom we might give offense" upon building walls. Oftentimes in relationships, walls create inequality and hatred. Today, choose to build bridges instead of walls, and you will be blessed with good relationships.

PEOPLE ARE LONELY BECAUSE THEY
BUILD WALLS INSTEAD OF BRIDGES.

JOSEPH FORT NEWTON

DETERMINED CHOICE

"*P*lease understand that there are times when the body, for some reason or another, will spontaneously abort the fetus."

The world seemed to stop dead still for Jim and Donna as they listened to her physician. Donna, in just her fourth month, had begun to hemorrhage earlier in the day. When they came to Dr. Joseph's, office they were concerned; now, they were becoming very frightened.

"It is nothing that you have done or not done," continued Dr. Joseph, "but, we want to send you down for an immediate ultrasound to see how things are doing. I want you to know that if your body has decided to abort the fetus, it is for a good reason. But, let's wait until we know for sure."

GIVE YOUR SERVANT A DISCERNING HEART.

1 KINGS 3:9

With those parting words, Jim and Donna headed to the lab for the ultrasound test.

"Jim, Jim, can you see the baby? He's right there! He's okay, he's okay!" shouted Donna as soon as the technician showed them the form of their baby on the monitor, and they could clearly see its heart beating. The baby was indeed still alive; Donna's body had not aborted him. They were overwhelmed with relief.

Five months later their first son was born, and another miracle took place as he survived complications during the birth. Upon finally bringing their "miracle boy" home, they both agreed that God must have something really special in store for him.

Where had such faith come from? Determined choice, perhaps. As Oswald Chambers once said, "Faith is deliberate confidence in the character of God whose ways you may not understand at the time."[25]

HOPE IS FAITH HOLDING OUT
ITS HANDS IN THE DARK.

GEORGE ILES

As God Is My
Witness . . .

*T*o some, one of the most devastatingly funny episodes of television in the 1980s came from the comedy series *WKRP in Cincinnati*. Set in a small Ohio radio station at Thanksgiving, the plot involved a promotion in which the advertising manager decided to give away free turkeys to customers patronizing a local shopping center.

As they planned a giveaway circus, complete with airplane fly-overs and a live remote news setup, the staff was certain this would be their most successful promotional campaign ever.

But the station manager soon learned that, once again, he had overestimated the basic intelligence of his ad manager. *WKRP* fans will long remember the chaotic radio broadcast as terrified customers and shopkeepers ran screaming, dodging the live turkeys which were, in the words of the quivering news reporter, "dropping like bags of wet cement," as they were tossed from the airplane circling above the shopping center.

And few viewers will forget the stunned look on the station manager's face as his abashed and bewildered ad man held his hand up to swear, "As God is my witness, *I thought turkeys could fly!*"

The lesson we learn from this is that we may not know everything, so it's good to ask questions. And that's where God's wonderful gift of humility comes in. Don't be ashamed to find out what you don't know— just remember the turkeys.

THE PATH OF HUMILITY
IS THE PATH TO GLORY.

ROBERT HAROLD SCHULLER

THE EFFECTIVE OPTIMIST

A Hasidic story tells of Rabbi Naftali of Ropchitz, known for his persistence—and for his wit. One day, he remained in the synagogue an entire morning, praying that the rich would give more of their money to the poor.

When he returned home, his wife asked him, "Were you successful with your prayer?"

Rabbi Naftali answered with a smile, "I am halfway there!" His wife looked puzzled, so he continued, "Oh, yes, the poor have agreed to accept!"[26]

Optimism is one of the greatest gifts of human nature. Many of civilization's achievements can be traced—not to the highest intellects or talents—but to perseverance and positive thinking.

It's a misconception that optimism requires no more than a sunny assumption that things will be fine.

> REJOICING IN HOPE, PATIENT IN TRIBULATION, CONTINUING STEADFASTLY IN PRAYER.
>
> ROMANS 12:12 NKJV

Real optimists rarely sit back and wait. Attitude is only the beginning.

George Bernard Shaw once said, "People are always blaming their circumstances for what they are. I don't believe in circumstances. The people who get on in this world are the people who get up and look for the circumstances they want, and if they can't find them . . . they make them!"

Positive thinkers can't guarantee that things will go well, but they use every available resource to help make their goal a reality, including—and especially—prayer.

There is no more hopeful time than morning, when the day is new and full of promise. What are your challenges today? Pray to God in the morning, and ask for His help in pointing out the hidden opportunities. It's the first step to becoming an effective optimist.

PRAYER CAN DO ANYTHING
THAT GOD CAN DO.

EDWARD McKENDREE BOUNDS

EVERYDAY GRACE

*I*n his book *Come As You Are,* G. Peter Fleck relates a satire of the Sermon on the Mount that could easily occur today:

Then Jesus took His disciples up the mountain and gathering them around Him, He taught them, saying:

"Blessed are the poor in spirit, for theirs is the kingdom of heaven.

Blessed are the meek.

Blessed are they that mourn.

Blessed are the merciful.

Blessed are they who thirst for justice.

Blessed are you who are persecuted.

Blessed are you when you suffer.

Be glad and rejoice for great is your reward in Heaven, and remember what I am telling you."

Then Simon Peter said, "Do we have to write this down?". . .

And James said, "Will we have a test on this?". . .

And Bartholomew said, "Do we have to turn this in?". . .

And John said, "The other disciples didn't have to learn this." . . .

And Judas said, "What does this have to do with real life?"[27]

In the author's words, "Grace had gone unrecognized."

Indeed, we experience God's grace regularly—but do we recognize it? Fleck defines grace as ". . . a blessing that is unexpected . . . that brings a sense of the divine order of things into our lives."

Do you notice the *everyday grace* in life? It comes at the oddest moments—in the words of children, a good idea when needed, or a call from a friend when it's least expected.

As you prepare for a new day, open your eyes to everyday grace. It is God's way of saying, "I am here."

GRACE IS A CERTAIN BEGINNING
OF GLORY IN US.

SAINT THOMAS AQUINAS

THE WORK OF
THE POTTER

I WENT DOWN TO THE POTTER'S
HOUSE, AND, BEHOLD, HE WROUGHT
A WORK ON THE WHEELS.

JEREMIAH 18:3 KJV

*H*ave you ever watched potters begin to shape vessels? It is a most amazing sight, because the potters will only succeed if they get the unformed chunk of clay in the exact center of the wheel. Once the clay is centered, the skill of the potters can be realized.

The potters carefully wet their hands, select the clay, and place it on the wheel. As they begin to turn the wheel, the lumps in the clay are revealed. Spinning the wheel faster, they smooth out the lumps, and the clay begins to take on an unruffled appearance.

This is just the first part of the task. We now see them shape the mass of clay so that its heart is perfectly aligned with the very center of the wheel. This requires both strength and a loving, delicate touch. This "centering" is the most important step in the preparation process, because it gives the piece strength and integrity.

Our spiritual walk with God is just like this. We begin as a hunk of clay with many lumps, and through God's grace and skill, we are transformed into beautiful, strong vessels for the Kingdom. But we must align our very heart with the center of God's will. God is always at work in our lives, especially during the times of proper preparation.

Henry Ward Beecher said, "We are always on the anvil; by trials God is shaping us for higher things."[28] Of this you can rest assured: When you allow God to shape you, He will always use you for good.

BE SIMPLE; TAKE OUR
LORD'S HAND AND
WALK THROUGH THINGS.

FATHER ANDREW

Make Me a Channel of Blessing

Can you imagine a professional football tackle pitching for a major league baseball game? He might be able to throw the ball with speed because he is strong and in great physical condition, but he won't have a great knuckle ball or a split finger ball that just makes it over the inside corner of the plate for a strike. He isn't equipped to play that position in that setting.

While all athletes go through extensive training to strengthen their God-given talents, each player actually is a specialist in his or her sport of choice. There are rare occasions where an athlete can change from one sport to another and still play well. But even that athlete will function better in one particular sport, playing one particular position.

So, too, are our spiritual gifts. Each of us has talents, and God has asked us to be channels of blessing to others. We may be able to do many things—even do them well—but we will find the greatest fulfillment and success when we use our gifts the way God intended they be used.

Being prepared for the work God has called us to do begins with knowing what our gifts are and then surrendering our gifts totally to Him. Knowing what we have to offer to our family, friends, and community helps us discover our unique place in God's garden.

> Channels only, blessed Master,
> But with all Thy wondrous power
> Flowing thro' us, Thou canst use us
> Ev-'ry day and ev-'ry hour.[29]

GOD'S GIFTS PUT MAN'S BEST DREAMS TO SHAME.

ELIZABETH BARRETT BROWNING

Clinging Vines

Scuppernong vines are parasites that grow up the trunks of and cling to healthy, firmly rooted trees in the southern United States. Walnut-sized, dark-skinned wild grapes grow on these vines and are used to make jams and jellies, and some southerners use their hull skins for cobbler pies. The fruit produced by these vines has served as an inexpensive treat to poor families in the South for many years. In recent years scuppernongs have become more popular and can be purchased at stores all over the South.

"I AM THE VINE, YOU ARE THE BRANCHES; HE WHO ABIDES IN ME, AND I IN HIM, HE BEARS MUCH FRUIT; FOR APART FROM ME YOU CAN DO NOTHING."

JOHN 15:5 NASB

As beautiful, diverse, and tasty as the scuppernong is, it cannot survive on its own. It needs the life support of well-established trees to cling to and draw its nourishment from. Should the scuppernong vine be pulled away from its host tree, it will dry up and stop producing fruit.

Like the scuppernong, we cannot survive without total dependency on God. Without

Him, we have no true life source, no lifeline, no nourishment; and we cannot produce good fruit.

We can, however, learn to cling to the Lord by surrendering ourselves to Him. We can draw nourishment through Bible study, prayer, worship, service, and heartfelt obedience. Like the scuppernong, clinging to our Source will help us grow healthy and produce much good fruit.

PEOPLE CAN MEET SUPERFICIAL
NEEDS. BUT ONLY GOD CAN
MEET OUR DEEP NEEDS.

FORRESTER BARRINGTON

Don't Blame
the Lettuce!

HE WHO PLANTS AND HE WHO
WATERS ARE ONE; BUT EACH WILL
RECEIVE HIS OWN REWARD
ACCORDING TO HIS OWN LABOR.

1 Corinthians 3:8 NASB

*O*ne evening, several college students spread Limburger cheese on the upper lip of a sleeping fraternity brother.

Upon awakening, the young man sniffed, looked around, and said, "This room stinks!"

He then walked into the hall and said, "This hall stinks!"

Leaving the dormitory, he exclaimed, "The whole world stinks!"

How long do you think it took for that sleepy student to discover the problem was right under his own nose?

It is easy, and maybe even our nature, to find fault with the outside world while remaining blind to the ways we contribute to the problem. Are there times when *we're* the problem?

When you plant lettuce, if it does not grow well, you don't blame the lettuce. You look for reasons it is not doing well. It may need fertilizer, or more water, or less sun. You never blame the lettuce. Yet if we have problems with our friends or our family, we often blame them. But in reality, if we know how to take care of them, they will grow well, like the lettuce. Blaming has no positive effect at all, nor does trying to persuade using reason and argument.

In the garden of our relationships, it is our job as caretakers to seek the most nurturing climate and soil. We must uproot the weeds of negativity and self-right-eousness and protect the tender plants from the heat of jealousy and harsh wind of anger. When we apply God's love and care to our dealings with the important people in our lives, our relationships will most certainly grow and flourish.

SEE EVERYTHING; OVERLOOK
A GREAT DEAL; CORRECT
A LITTLE.

POPE JOHN XXIII

SONLIGHT IN
MY GARDEN

Martha badgered Johnny all year to plant her a garden. Finally, he agreed. Together they tilled the soil, preparing it with the best additives, including peat moss, landscape mix, soil conditioners, and bark mulch.

GROW IN THE
GRACE AND
KNOWLEDGE OF
OUR LORD AND
SAVIOR JESUS
CHRIST.

2 PETER 3:18

Martha disliked the flowers in her local nursery, so she begged Johnny to let her order some unique varieties out of a mail order catalog. Gingerly, she selected each one, often choosing the most expensive plants. *It will be the prettiest yard in the neighborhood,* she thought. *No one can match these beauties.*

The tender plants arrived in the mail, and Martha began working immediately. She planted and watered; she fertilized; she watched; and she waited. But nothing happened. One by one, the leaves turned yellow and began to wilt. By the end of spring, not one plant remained. They all had shriveled and died.

Martha wrote a scathing letter to the mail order nursery demanding her money back.

Two weeks later, she received this reply:

Madam, your letter indicated you planted your flowers in a beautiful shady area and fed them the best nutrients possible. Your flowers failed to grow for the following reason: You planted them in the wrong place. You ordered flowers that must face the sun. Although you took great care to prepare the soil, without exception, these particular plants will die without sunlight. Next time, please read the directions before ordering your flowers and planting your garden.

Our lives are like that. We may spend great amounts of care and money to make ourselves beautiful. But if we are not facing the Son, we will wilt and eventually die. No amount of expensive "additives" will take the place of adequate Sonlight in our souls.

FAILURE IS ONLY THE OPPORTUNITY TO BEGIN AGAIN MORE INTELLIGENTLY.

HENRY FORD

BLOOM WHERE YOU ARE TRANSPLANTED

A young couple moved to a new city, far from family and friends. The movers arrived; the couple unpacked their belongings; and the husband started his job the following week. Each day when he arrived home, his wife greeted him at the door with a new complaint.

"It's so hot here."

"The neighbors are unfriendly."

"The house is too small."

"The kids are driving me crazy."

YOU WILL BE LIKE A WELL-WATERED GARDEN, LIKE A SPRING WHOSE WATERS NEVER FAIL.

ISAIAH 58:11

And each afternoon, her husband would hold her gently and listen to her gripes. "I'm sorry," he would say. "What can I do to help?"

His wife would soften and dry her tears, only to begin the same scenario the next afternoon.

One evening her husband walked through the front door with a beautiful flowering plant. He found a choice spot in the backyard and planted it. "Honey," he said. "Every time you feel discontented, I want you to go and look at your garden. Picture yourself as that little flowering plant. And watch your garden grow."

Every week he brought home a new tree, flowering shrub, or rose bush and planted it in the backyard. His wife cut some flowers from the growing plants and took them to a neighbor. Each morning she watered the garden and measured its progress. Friendships grew with other women in her block, and they asked her for gardening help. Soon, they were seeking spiritual advice as well.

By the end of the next year, the couples' yard looked like a *Better Homes & Gardens* magazine feature.

Our Heavenly Father knows that we must all learn to bloom where we are transplanted. With His wise, loving touch, we will not only flourish, but we can also produce the ever-blooming fruit of love, kindness, and contentment.

> FOR AFTER ALL, THE BEST
> THING ONE CAN DO WHEN IT'S
> RAINING IS TO LET IT RAIN.
>
> HENRY WADSWORTH LONGFELLOW

WORKING THE SOIL

THE LORD IS NIGH UNTO THEM THAT ARE OF A BROKEN HEART.

PSALM 34:18 KJV

*E*ven though her husband had been gone for months now, Nancy still missed Bill immensely. Whenever her loneliness became too great, she would head for the garage and her gardening tools. She and Bill had a garden for as long as the grandchildren could remember, and she was determined that they would still have a garden even after Bill was gone. Besides, it gave her life purpose, and it seemed as if Bill were right there with her as she turned the soil, planted the seeds, watered the seedlings, weeded, and encouraged the plants to grow.

As she worked, she remembered the times they had worked side-by-side. She recalled how she liked to see the muscles in Bill's forearms ripple as he pulled weeds, how dark the dirt was against the tanned skin of the backs of his hands, and how he would always wipe the sweat from his face with a big red bandanna. Without much effort, she could even see again how the sunlight bounced off his wide-brimmed straw hat and the way his eyes would sparkle with anticipation as he spoke of the harvest to come.

She seemed to feel him nearby as she worked in the garden, and she often quietly murmured, "Bill, I know we will have some good tomatoes this year."

It is hard to experience more contentment than when you see the rewards of your work. Life is much the same in that sense: whether one is tending a garden, raising a child, or growing a marriage—it takes work. Whether alone or with a loved one, we always have the company of a special Companion throughout life's journey. Just ask Nancy.

HE IS A WISE MAN WHO
DOES NOT GRIEVE FOR
THE THINGS WHICH HE
HAS NOT, BUT REJOICES
FOR THOSE WHICH HE HAS.

EPICTEUS

SMALL YET TALL

*D*avid was a shepherd boy who faced the fierce Philistine giant, Goliath. His enormous opponent was armed and seemed to be well prepared to meet his enemy in battle. Goliath had seen many battles before. He was a warrior, but often he relied solely on his size and ferocity to win the battle before weapons were even drawn. He was the Philistines' icon of strength.

Mocking laughter could be heard all over the countryside when this powerful, tall, well-developed warrior stood there facing a boy. How could this be? Surely Goliath had the upper hand. He was the strongest and the best the Philistines had.

What did David bring to this battle? He was a boy, untrained in the weapons of warfare. He did not stand a chance. He was too young. For David's people, this seemed to be yet another disaster waiting to happen.

IN ALL THESE THINGS WE OVERWHELM-INGLY CONQUER THROUGH HIM WHO LOVED US.

ROMANS 8:37 NASB

While Goliath mocked God, David worshipped the Lord. Goliath was smug in his sure victory; David asked

God for a miracle. Goliath trusted his size and strength to save him; David relied on Someone far bigger and stronger. Though small, David trusted in a mighty God. And in the end, one tiny stone defeated the giant.

For thousands of years, tiny seeds planted in the cold, dark earth have yielded bumper crops of vegetation, towering trees, and every imaginable flowering plant. Faith plants a seed and looks for the harvest. David threw a stone and looked for a victory.

FAITH IS NOT BELIEVING THAT
GOD CAN, BUT THAT GOD WILL.

ABRAHAM LINCOLN

UPROOT THE TREE

$\mathcal{A}$fter months of searching, a lawyer and his wife bought a house. They loved everything about it, especially the shady backyard. The contract went well—until the inspector finished his examination of the foundation.

"You have a tree growing too close to the house," he said. "If you don't remove it, the roots will eventually erode the foundation and cause it to shift. First, you'll see cracks on the inside walls and then a major break on the outside brick structure. If you uproot the tree now and start watering the foundation regularly, the problem will correct itself—a minor cost of five hundred dollars for tree removal."

The lawyer's wife grew angry. "The reason we wanted this house was because of the trees, especially that one! We'll take our chances!"

So they moved in. They planted an expensive garden underneath the tree and enjoyed the shade all year long. One day, the lawyer

THERE IS A TIME . . . TO PLANT AND A TIME TO UPROOT.

ECCLESIASTES 3:1-2

noticed large cracks on the inside walls, and a jagged line followed the two-inch split in the outside brick wall—only a few feet from the tree roots.

The disgusted lawyer listed the house for sale immediately, but no one would buy the home. Finally, two years later, a realtor found a buyer with one condition: the owners repair the house before the sale.

By this time, the foundation needed a complete restoration. The cost? Just over ten thousand dollars. Eager to move out, the lawyer paid the money and sold the house at a substantial loss.

Like the lawyer's shade tree, little problems in life often appear harmless. If we ignore God's warnings to pull them up by the roots, those problems will eventually grow large enough to erode our spiritual foundation. We can avoid needless costly mistakes by listening—and heeding—God's words.

HUMAN PROBLEMS ARE NEVER
GREATER THAN DIVINE SOLUTIONS.

ERWIN W. LUTZER

I FORGIVE YOU

GROW IN GRACE.

2 PETER 3:18 KJV

The cause of Jim's anger had long since been forgotten, but he continued to rail at his young son, Ricky. He couldn't seem to stop himself. He was just so frustrated with the boy. On and on he went until finally he had exhausted his anger, and then he immediately felt guilty for his behavior.

Looking deep into Ricky's tear-filled eyes, Jim said, "Son, I am so sorry that I lost my temper. I was wrong to scream at you, and I was wrong to become so angry regardless of your actions. Will you please forgive me?"

Without a moment's hesitation, Ricky responded, "It's all right, Dad; Jesus forgives you, and so do I!"

And then Ricky immediately launched himself into his father's arms for a hug. They remained that way for a couple of moments as the healing balm of forgiveness washed over them both. They had a special bond that was strong enough to stand the tests of parenting and growing up, a bond that was made stronger still by their shared faith. It seemed that Ricky's growing up was also forcing Jim to deal with his own childish behaviors and to make some changes.

Jim was acutely aware that his every action was scrutinized by his young son, and he wanted to be a good father. He asked God to help him be a good example. He still struggled with his temper and impatience, but he committed himself to change his behavior. The words of his young son humbled and encouraged him: "It's all right, Dad; Jesus forgives you, and so do I!" He heard again.

Worthy or not, we are forgiven if we ask.

IF GOD WERE NOT WILLING
TO FORGIVE SIN, HEAVEN
WOULD BE EMPTY.

GERMAN PROVERB

A FIRM FOUNDATION

The world's tallest tower stands in Toronto, Ontario, Canada. The first observation deck rises to 1,136 feet, and the second is even higher at 1,815 feet. Photographs and information located inside the tower help visitors comprehend the enormous undertaking of the project. Sixty-two tons of earth and shale were removed from fifty feet into the ground for laying the concrete that rises to the sky.

From 1972 to 1974, three thousand workers were at the tower site. Harnessed by safety ropes, some of the laborers dangled outside the giant for their finishing work. Remarkably, no one sustained injuries nor died on location.

Today a rapid elevator transports visitors upward for a breathtaking view of the city and all surrounding areas. Many believe it was well worth the money, time, and effort required to build the CN Tower.

"THE RAIN CAME DOWN, THE STREAMS ROSE, AND THE WINDS BLEW AND BEAT AGAINST THAT HOUSE; YET IT DID NOT FALL, BECAUSE IT HAD ITS FOUNDATION ON THE ROCK."

MATTHEW 7:25

We, too, need a good foundation for facing life each day. As we pray and spend time with our Heavenly Father, we are strengthening our spiritual foundation, our support base for life. We are able to see more from His point of view and not just our own. Thus we are not overwhelmed by whatever comes our way. When we feel we're hanging on the edge or suspended in mid-air, we can take courage in knowing He is holding us—firmly planted—in the palm of His hand. His foundation is strong and sure, and He will not crumble and fall.

FAITH IS THE CHRISTIAN'S FOUNDATION,
HOPE IS HIS ANCHOR, DEATH IS
HIS HARBOR, CHRIST IS HIS PILOT,
AND HEAVEN IS HIS COUNTRY.

JEREMY TAYLOR

SMELL THE ROSES

*I*n his book *Seasons of Life,* Charles Swindoll tells the following story about the defender of the theory of evolution, the famous biologist and devoted disciple of Darwin, Thomas Henry Huxley:

Having finished another series of public assaults against several truths Christians held sacred, Huxley was in a hurry the following morning to catch his train to the next city. He took one of Dublin's famous horse-drawn taxis and settled back with his eyes closed to rest himself for a few minutes. He assumed the driver had been told the destination by the motel doorman, so all he had said as he got in was, "Hurry . . . I'm almost late. *Drive fast!*" The horses lurched forward and galloped across Dublin at a vigorous pace. Before long Huxley glanced out the window and frowned as he realized they

LISTEN FOR GOD'S VOICE IN EVERYTHING YOU DO, EVERYWHERE YOU GO; HE'S THE ONE WHO WILL KEEP YOU ON TRACK.

PROVERBS 3:6 THE MESSAGE

were going west, *away* from the sun, not toward it.

Leaning forward, the scholar shouted, "Do you know where you are going?" Without looking back, the driver yelled a classic line, not meant to be humorous, "No, your honor! But I am driving *very* fast!"

As Rollo May, the contemporary psychologist, once admitted: "It is an old and ironic habit of human beings to run faster when we have lost our way."[30]

Garden-tending requires time, a slowing down of our breakneck speeds. Taking time to "smell the roses"—especially lingering near the fragrance of the Rose of Sharon—helps us to receive God's clear directions on where we are really headed in life. If we will head toward the Son with a listening ear and give up speeding to meaningless destinations, we will discover a purposeful life, filled with good things from the Master Gardener.

KIND THOUGHTS,
CONTENTMENT, PEACE OF MIND,
AND JOY FOR WEARY HOURS.

MARY HOWITT

RIPE CANTALOUPES

Rita and James could scarcely wait to pick the cantaloupes. The children had worked hard preparing the soil, planting, watering, pulling weeds, and keeping the bugs out of their garden. Now, with small cantaloupes on the vines, it had become pure torture to wait for the tender fruit to mature and grow.

Early on, they would venture out daily to see if things were growing yet. But every morning was an exercise in patience. All they could see was dirt—nothing but bare dirt!

Then one day, tiny green shoots had shoved aside the earth and were emerging from the soil. Fuzzy cantaloupe vines began to spread across the small hills at the rear of the garden—soon to bear melons.

"Dad, this one's ready to pick; I just know it is!" James cried.

"Nope, I'm afraid not," Dad replied. "It may look big enough to pick, but it's not ripe yet. Don't you see how green it still is?"

Once Dad left, they could not wait anymore. They picked the melon. Alas, just as Dad had warned, the hard melon was far from ripe. When they told him later, he quietly laughed.

The next week, he came to them and said, "Hey, would you two like some fresh, homegrown cantaloupe?" Their faces lit up with excitement, and the trio ventured to the garden where Dad pointed out two beautifully ripened melons for them to pick.

Rita grinned at her father between bites of melon and said, "It sure tastes better when we wait for the right time to pick the cantaloupe, doesn't it, Dad?"

Being patient for God's perfect timing can be difficult. But it's always worth the wait.

GOD DELAYS BUT
DOESN'T FORGET.

SPANISH PROVERB

BUMPER CROP

*D*orothy wasn't allowed to plant a garden outside the townhouse they rented, so she decided to do the next best thing. She bought large pots and created a container garden on her patio.

One evening while she relaxed on the patio, her husband said, "Look! Our neighbor has tomatoes already. Why don't we?"

Much to her amazement, her neighbor had an abundance of fat green tomatoes covering her vines. All that Dorothy had growing were the tiny yellow flowers that promised fruit.

Dorothy had babied her plant by gently positioning it up the rungs of its tomato cage as it grew. She had judiciously showered it with water and moved the pots around for the best sunshine. Yet, all she had was a profusion of vines.

Dorothy searched through her gardening books and discovered that she needed to pinch back staked tomato plants. Pinching helps the plant focus its energy on producing its fruit instead of merely growing taller.

Many of us are like Dorothy's tomato plant. We love showing the abundant leaves of our spiritual insights. We take pride in how we are climbing the rungs of increased Bible knowledge. But do we only promise fruit? Or do we, instead, apply what we've learned to our actions and focus our energy on producing quality fruit?

When we pinch back our self-centeredness and concentrate on Christ, we might even grow a bumper crop of fruit to God's glory.

FIRST THE BLADE, AND THEN THE EAR,
THEN THE FULL CORN SHALL APPEAR.
LORD OF HARVEST, GRANT THAT WE,
WHOLE-SOME GRAIN AND PURE MAY BE.

HENRY ALFORD

THE LOST CUCUMBER

"Wow, Dad can you believe the size of this cucumber!" Danny nearly screamed as they walked through the family garden. They had been gone on vacation for over three weeks, and now the garden was somewhat overgrown. Since no one had been tending to it, many of the vegetables that should have been picked, remained on the vine. One such vegetable was this large cucumber. It was the largest cucumber Danny had ever seen; but when he looked closer, he found that it was more golden than green, and it had rotten spots on the bottom where it lay touching the earth.

"Dad, we can't use this; it's not fit to eat. We needed to be here at least a week ago!"

THE HARVEST IS PAST, THE SUMMER HAS ENDED.

JEREMIAH 8:20

Danny's father smiled at his son's exaggerated reaction and then remarked, "Yep, you're right. It is neat to see a cucumber this big, but we cannot use it for anything. We weren't here to watch for this cucumber, and now it's too late to pick it and to enjoy it."

Like the lost cucumber, life is often filled with "missed opportunities." The harvest of souls for the Kingdom of God requires we be watching and ready. Seeds sometimes bear fruit when we least expect it. We may fail to see opportunities because our attention is on things other than Him. Those opportunities become "could have," "should have," or "would have" regrets in our lives.

FOUR THINGS COME NOT BACK—
THE SPOKEN WORD, THE SPED
ARROW, THE PAST LIFE, AND THE
NEGLECTED OPPORTUNITY.

UNKNOWN

EMPTY

> I WENT PAST THE . . . VINEYARD OF THE
> MAN WHO LACKS JUDGMENT; THORNS
> HAD COME UP EVERYWHERE, THE
> GROUND WAS COVERED WITH WEEDS,
> AND THE STONE WALL WAS IN RUINS.
>
> PROVERBS 24:30-31

He was an angry man, cynical and mistrusting of others. He had been married seven different times in his life. He had a fair-sized nest egg put aside, and he was only a few years from retirement. But he did not seem to look forward to it.

His name was Charlie, and those who had known him early in his life said that he had not always been so difficult to get along with. They said that when he was young, he was just irresponsible. But as he grew older and his life became characterized by failed relationships, he became bitter and angry.

Charlie's neighbors watched as his orchard suffered from neglect. The fence, fallen down in many places, was overgrown with wild vines. The untended orange trees grew ragged and without uniform shape, and down the rows between the trees, the weeds were knee-high, in some places, waist high. Rotting oranges were in evidence deep in the weeds. It had been a long time since anyone had paid attention to this orchard.

Charlie's life was like his orchard. In his book *Man, the Dwelling Place of God*, A. W. Tozer wrote, "The untended garden will soon be overrun with weeds; the heart that fails to cultivate truth and root out error will shortly be a theological wilderness."[31]

Do you know a "Charlie," whose spiritual garden only yields a bitter harvest? Ask the Master Gardener to use you to plant seeds of love and to send other laborers to help this person enter a new season of hope and joy.

GOD ALWAYS GIVE HIS VERY
BEST TO THOSE WHO LEAVE
THE CHOICE WITH HIM.

JAMES HUDSON TAYLOR

FOREVER FAITHFUL

*J*im Cymbala was a former college basketball player working in the business world of downtown Manhattan when his life took a dramatic turn. He had majored in sociology in college and had never been to Bible college, much less a seminary school, when he took the pastorate of a small church in New Jersey, at the urging of his father-in-law.

He did not consider himself a gifted or talented minister and preacher, but he was faithful to his father-in-law. And, when his father-in-law asked him to also serve as pastor for a second church, he again agreed. Eventually he and his wife determined that they could not pastor two churches, so they decided to stay with the second church—the smaller and less secure one. Over time he became discouraged at the lack of success.

Of that time he wrote, "I despaired at the thought that my life might slip by without seeing God show Himself mightily on our behalf."[32]

Prayer and persistence paid off. Jim Cymbala still serves as the pastor of that same church, the one that had less than thirty members when he took the pastorate more than twenty-five years ago.

Today, the church has more than six thousand members and has started no less than twenty other churches.

It also has a pretty good choir led by Mrs. Jim Cymbala—the Grammy Award-winning Brooklyn Tabernacle Choir. The church and the choir provide astonishing evidence of the faithfulness of God. It is a faithfulness that benefits all of God's children, including you!

WHATEVER IS WORTH DOING AT ALL, IS WORTH DOING WELL.

LORD CHESTERFIELD

MIRACLE OF LOVE

$\mathcal{A}$ phone call one day changed May and Joe Lemke's life. Someone requested her help with a foster child. Her devotion as a nurse, combined with this English woman's gentle and tender love for children, had earned her the reputation of miracle worker, one which she would need for the challenge facing her that day.

The six-month-old infant boy named Leslie had been born severely retarded and with cerebral palsy. His doctors had removed both of his badly damaged eyes. May worked tirelessly and faithfully week after week, month after month, with virtually no change in the vegetable-like body.

> "THIS HAPPENED SO THAT THE WORK OF GOD MIGHT BE DISPLAYED IN HIS LIFE."
>
> JOHN 9:3

She and her husband, now well into their sixties, continued their rituals of exercise, feeding, talking, and even playing music recordings for Leslie. When he was thirteen, they bought a piano, and May began to play simple songs for him to hear. Still, no communication, no expression, nothing. But as May began to pray for God to give Leslie a talent, the parents noticed an intensity with which he listened to music.

Then one day at age sixteen, Leslie dragged himself to the piano in his room, never having walked before, never having played a single note before, and played Tchaikovsky's "Piano Concert no. 1" flawlessly.

The Lemkes discovered he could play anything after hearing it just one time. The miracles continued, and one day they heard his rich, baritone voice singing "How Great Thou Art." He learned to talk, to walk alone, and to eat by himself.[33]

With God, nothing is impossible.

IMPOSSIBLE IS A WORD ONLY FOUND
IN THE DICTIONARY OF FOOLS.

NAPOLEON BONAPARTE

BUTTERFLY WINGS

[LOVE] ALWAYS PROTECTS, ALWAYS
TRUSTS, ALWAYS HOPES, ALWAYS
PERSEVERES. LOVE NEVER FAILS.

1 CORINTHIANS 13:7-8

*H*ow do you find your place in the sun when planted in the middle of fame? In *Seasons of Life*, Charles Swindoll writes this of Anne and Charles Lindbergh:

> Anne was shy and delicate. Butterfly like. When she became Mrs. Charles Lindbergh, Anne could have easily been eclipsed by her husband's shadow. She wasn't, however. The love that bound the two together for the next forty-seven years was tough love, mature love, tested by triumph and tragedy alike.

Anne describes how Charles Lindbergh's love freed her to become a woman of beauty:

> To be deeply in love is, of course, a great liberating force and the most common experience that frees. . . . Ideally, both members of a couple in love free each other to new and different worlds. I was no exception to the general

rule. The sheer fact of finding myself loved was unbelievable and changed my world, my feelings about life and myself. I was given confidence, strength, and almost a new character. The man I was to marry believed in me and what I could do, and consequently I found I could do more than I realized.[34]

The security of her husband's love released Anne to discover her own talents and gifts and to "emerge from that cocoon of shyness a beautiful, ever delicate butterfly" who would touch many lives.

Some marriages create cocoons of fear and timidity in their spouses. They may squeeze their partners from silk-like safety zones prematurely. Some spouses hover in the garden with a net, or treat their mates like a specimen under glass—afraid their beloved butterfly will discover wings and fly away.

But love, gentle and patient, knows that fragile butterflies belong to the Lord. And when they are given true wings, they never fly far from home.

WE BLOSSOM UNDER
PRAISE LIKE FLOWERS IN SUN
AND DEW; WE OPEN,
WE REACH, WE GROW.

GERHARD E. FROST

PALM SALAD

*T*he honeymooning couple crossed the long bridge from mainland Florida to Cedar Keys, a small island near central Florida. It was an exciting ride along dirt roads lined with huge trees permanently bent in the same direction from the last major hurricane that hit the island with gale force winds. Friends had recommended a restaurant on the island, where they could try the freshest and best seafood in Florida along with a bowl of the house specialty, palm salad. The drive was all the more pleasant because of the sweet anticipation of a good meal.

> THE RIGHT-EOUS MAN WILL FLOURISH LIKE THE PALM TREE.
>
> PSALM 92:12 NASB

The presentation was exquisite; the food was delicious. The curious couple asked the waiter what part of the palm was used and how it was harvested. The islander explained that the scrub palm had to be cut so the leaves, thorns, and any parasites were removed. Using a machete to top the palm out to expose the deep part of its core, the harvester cuts deep inside the pulp to remove the heart of the palm, which is used for the salad. Such a deliberate and difficult act is performed many times a day so guests can enjoy the succulent palm salad.

Before the heart of the palm was discovered, no one could enjoy its tasty delight. No one knew it even existed. What a shame to miss out on something so enjoyable!

May the eyes of our hearts be opened so that we can see—and savor—the blessings around us.

EXAMINE THE CONTENTS,
NOT THE BOTTLE.

THE TALMUD

SEASONS

*A*t a dinner party honoring Albert Einstein, a student asked the great scientist, "What do you actually do as a profession?"

Mr. Einstein said, "I devote myself to the study of physics."

The student then exclaimed, "You mean that you're still studying physics? I finished mine last year."[35]

One of the very real temptations of life is to divide it into seasons and then think of each season as an end within itself. Students may think of the high school diploma as the goal and not relate it to what they want to do with their lives. Graduates may get the jobs of their choice and never consider that other jobs could be in their future.

A MAN REAPS
WHAT HE SOWS.

GALATIANS 6:7

How often have you seen a young man and woman become engaged to be married, then spend thousands of dollars and hundreds of hours preparing for the wedding, with little or no preparation for the years of marriage ahead? Or, the couple may look forward with great anticipation to the birth of a child, with no plan for proper parenting.

The Garden of Life is a continuing cycle of seasons and years. Those who reap the greatest harvests seem to look both backward and forward. They look to the past to glean from their experiences those things that will help solve the challenges of today. They look to the future to decide which seeds they should plant today to help them attain their goals for the future.

God is present in every segment of our lives, coaxing us to learn from both our experiences and goals, so that our gardens will reach their full potential.

IF YOU DON'T KNOW WHERE
YOU ARE GOING, ANY ROAD
WILL GET YOU THERE.

UNKNOWN

GREENER GRASS?

THOSE WHO PLOW EVIL AND THOSE
WHO SOW TROUBLE REAP IT.

JOB 4:8

A young man, having just finished college, landed an extremely well-paying position. He worked hard, watched others, and learned from them. He loved his wife, and his family grew. But soon he traded family time for the boardroom. He was bright and ambitious, eager to climb the corporate ladder and grasp for success. Within a few years he had risen to a top position in his company.

Suddenly others began to flock around this young wizard for professional advice—and for favors. Coworkers bribed, clients begged, and female friends flirted. The young man, eager to please and overwhelmed by the sudden attention, was blind to what was happening to him. He used his power unwisely and made some wrong financial decisions. He neglected his family and allowed seeds of discontent to grow in his heart. From his perspective, nothing but weeds grew in his garden.

In a moment of weakness and bad judgment, the young executive fell. He succumbed to temptation and ended up disgracing his family, quitting his job, and ultimately losing his integrity. Friends tried to help restore him, but he turned away from them. His family offered forgiveness, but the man could not forgive himself. He died a few years later, an alcoholic and a broken man.

The grass may look greener, and the flowers may seem more beautiful in another garden, but there's no place like the soil where we have been planted. God knows exactly what we need. He has given us all the right ingredients for a well-watered, successful life that honors Him.

IT IS NOT ENOUGH TO
HAVE GREAT QUALITIES;
ONE MUST MAKE GOOD
USE OF THEM.

FRANÇOIS, DUC DE LA
ROCHEFOUCAULD

A Lifetime to Learn

Orville was nearly seventy-four years old and had been in poor health for the past ten years. Early in life he had been a robust man, working from dawn to dusk. But now, the years had caught up with him, and he tired easily—to the point that he required frequent naps throughout the day when he really felt bad. This bothered him.

DOES NOT LONG LIFE BRING UNDER-STANDING?

JOB 12:12

He was visiting with two of his sons and reminiscing about the choices and decisions he had made throughout his life. Off and on, his voice quivered, and tears welled up in his eyes as he spoke of critical times in his life where certain decisions were beneficial for the family and others had caused great hardship.

He spoke of the time he left a secure, steady job to venture into a family business. The venture did not work out, and Orville and his young family struggled for years to dig out from under the mountain of debt that resulted. He also spoke of the time the family faced a mandatory move, and God guided them to the best choice of cities to relocate their home.

There were many more memories shared that afternoon. As the day wore on, the shadows lengthened in the room, and Orville's eyes closed for another of his brief naps. The two sons quietly remarked to one another that the knowledge learned in a lifetime is very hard to pass on. However, they promised to learn from Dad's mistakes and to copy his successes. In short, they vowed to love life as he did and to remain faithful to family and faith as he had.

THE WIND OF GOD IS ALWAYS BLOWING . . .
BUT YOU MUST HOIST YOUR SAIL.

FRANÇOIS FÉNELON

Fresh Rain

It had been a very hot and dry month, and the wheat fields were dusty and forlorn-looking. The uncultivated plains, scattered with sagebrush and dotted by tumbleweeds, seemed to bake in the afternoon sun. The sky stretched overhead, a brassy but deep blue. What few clouds there were seemed to dangle from the sky in shapeless masses of wispy white. But when Don looked low in the sky, just above the horizon, he saw a darker line of clouds.

His wife, Eleanor, stepped out the back door of their home to check on her garden. It had been so dry this summer that she had had to water three and four times a day to keep the snap beans, tomatoes, cucumbers, corn, and rhubarb from dying. As she surveyed her garden, she felt a hint of cooler air on her cheek. Glancing to the west, she saw that the light, wispy clouds of earlier in the day were being replaced by a growing line of towering thunderclouds heavy with much-needed rain.

I WILL GIVE YOU RAIN IN DUE SEASON, AND THE LAND SHALL YIELD HER INCREASE.

LEVITICUS 26:4 KJV

Later that day, Don bounded up the walk toward the house; he couldn't help but laugh and raise his face to the gentle rain. Earlier it had been heavy, with loud thunder; now, it was a gentle, soaking rain—one that would replenish wells and nourish wheat fields. Skipping around the corner of the house, he headed for the garden to find Eleanor. Taking deep breaths, he savored the smell of a fresh prairie rain on the well-tended soil of a garden.

Sure enough, he found her there, walking in her garden and thanking the Father for His ever-flowing blessings.

In the midst of difficult times in your life, remember to wait on the Lord. He will bring the much-awaited refreshing rain to your dry and thirsty soul.

IT AIN'T NO USE PUTTING UP
YOUR UMBRELLA TILL IT RAINS.

ALICE CALDWELL RICE

GROWING IN WISDOM

A WISE MAN WILL HEAR AND
INCREASE IN LEARNING, AND
A MAN OF UNDERSTANDING
WILL ACQUIRE WISE COUNSEL.

PROVERBS 1:5 NASB

*A*fter their wedding, the young couple prepared for their move from Ireland to America. It meant leaving their families behind and starting from scratch in a new country, but they were committed for the long haul. Even though many from their village came and settled close to them, it didn't take long for the newlyweds to realize that the man's trade would not allow him to provide for his family. What could have been the justification for a speedy retreat back to Dublin was, instead, the fuel that fired the determination to learn a new skill and prove he could provide for his family against all odds.

He and his wife agreed that Christ would be their Strength and Guide for the uphill battle that lay ahead. They decided that until a new skill was mastered, everything else had to take a back seat except their love and devotion to God and to each other.

The man bought a used typewriter, an adding machine, and several textbooks. After his regular job ended every day, he would sit until the wee hours of the next morning, studying, pecking away at both machines until he had taught himself how to type proficiently and how to do the work of a master accountant.

His work became so well known that for the rest of his life he was in constant demand. It was said that his work was the finest in the land. He and his family lived very comfortable lives, and he left a legacy to his children and others of a man who was willing to listen, learn, and grow in wisdom.

GENIUS IS 1 PERCENT
INSPIRATION AND
99 PERCENT PERSPIRATION.

THOMAS ALVA EDISON

In the Winter of My Heart

It was already winter in the Szuber family, even though autumn's leaves had not yet fallen. They were grieving.

When the car Patti Szuber was riding in hit a rock wall in Knoxville, Tennessee, and careened onto the road, rolling several times, the twenty-two-year-old beauty was killed.

Patti was an organ donor, and her family could choose who would be the recipient of her heart—an unknown person on the national waiting list or someone they knew. On the national list, in slot #2,935, was Chester Szuber, Patti's father. He had undergone three open-heart surgeries and two angioplasties and had lived with life-threatening heartbeat irregularities. Since his health was so serious, there were no real guarantees that Patti's heart would help Mr. Szuber. But he was willing and said, "It would be a joy to have Patti's heart."

Five hours and fifty-one minutes after Patti's heart stopped beating in Tennessee, it was functioning well in her father's chest. The transplant was successful.[36]

Winter, like the difficult season in the Szuber family, comes almost brutally at times, it seems. Nature, once vibrant with color and energy, sheds its life, leaving only bare branches—like bare hearts exposed. But God in His wisdom and divine plan knows that without death there can be no life. Seeds, just like His own Son, once dying, soon spring forth in another "body," breathing life and hope and second chances.

Those who understand this principle will find a true home in the Father's heart.

THE PILOT KNOWS THE UNKNOWN SEAS,
AND HE WILL BRING US THROUGH.

JOHN OXENHAM

SCHEDULED REST

Schedules. Sometimes we feel as though we're governed by to-do lists. The kitchen calendar overflows with notations: do this, go here, pick that up, buy this, deliver that, or mail this other thing. And just when we think we're on top of our lives, someone adds a new item to our to-do list.

Researchers say that Americans today are plagued with more stress-related health problems than any other generation in history. Stress is a contributing factor to heart disease and high blood pressure and has been linked to an increase in bad cholesterol and the worsening of arthritis.

[JESUS] SAID TO THEM, "COME WITH ME BY YOURSELVES TO A QUIET PLACE AND GET SOME REST."

MARK 6:31

How can we keep the daily pressures of life from becoming debilitating stress? God's solution has always been to take a day of rest. Return to the simple pleasures of the kitchen. The kitchen in our great-grandmothers' time was both the center of family activity and the center of rest. Family meals were made and shared around a common table. Conversation was the primary form of entertainment—not the television, radio, or compact disc player with headphones. Comforting aromas greeted family members throughout the day. And nothing could beat the smell of a chicken roasting in the oven for Sunday dinner.

So toss out the bottle of aspirin, and put your daily planner away for one day each week. Make sure everyone in the family knows that this will be a "scheduled" day of rest. Before you go to bed the night before, use your modern appliances to help give you a jump-start on the day. Pop some dough ingredients in the bread machine, and set the timer on the coffeepot. You'll awaken to the smell of freshly perked coffee and freshly baked bread. Those inviting aromas will make you want to linger in the kitchen—to chat, to laugh, to love, and to rest. God—and our great-grandmothers—will be pleased.

WE ALL NEED A SECRET HIDEAWAY
WHERE THE MIND CAN REST
AND THE SOUL CAN HEAL.

CHERIE RAYBURN

FIXER-UPPER

*R*uth and Bob had purchased what is called in real estate terms a "fixer-upper." Though the roof leaked in a few places and the building had been neglected for years, the two-story house was structurally sound. They were unskilled in remodeling techniques, yet the real-estate agent assured them that with a little effort and some paint and wallpaper, they could make this dwelling a comfortable home. They followed her advice and bought the house.

The first room they tackled was the kitchen. They pulled off scarred countertops and unhinged cabinet doors. They scrubbed, scraped, and peeled layers of dirt and accumulated paint and flooring. But two months later, with the kitchen stripped to the bare walls, Bob began a new job that required extensive travel. The time he could spend restoring the kitchen was cut in half.

Ruth now washed dinner dishes in the bathtub and prepared meals on a two-burner hot plate while her country kitchen lay in pieces, scattered throughout the basement. Impatient to have her kitchen finished, she began to complain, at first just to Bob, but later to anyone who would listen.

The Israelites were a lot like that. When God set them on the road to the Promised Land, they weren't pleased with the route or the time it was taking to get to their destination. Rather than focusing their eyes on God and His plan, the Israelites looked at their circumstances and complained. A trip that should have taken a few days turned into a forty-year marathon.

As Ruth stood in the center of her gutted kitchen, God reminded her of the consequences of the Israelites' bitter attitude. With renewed determination, she quickly turned her impatience and discouragement into hope and thanksgiving by focusing on God instead of her kitchen. After apologizing to her husband, Ruth renewed her effort to help Bob pull the scattered pieces of their kitchen together until the job was finished.

In the same way, we can transform our "fixer-upper" lives with patience and a Godly perspective. Do you have a room in your heart that needs a little "remodeling"?

A HANDFUL OF PATIENCE IS

WORTH MORE THAN

A BUSHEL OF BRAINS.

DUTCH PROVERB

SACRIFICE AT SEA

$\mathcal{C}$aptain Eddie Rickenbacker, a famous World War I pilot, was forced down into the Pacific Ocean while on an inspection trip in 1942. The plane, a B-17, stayed afloat just long enough for all aboard to get out. Amazingly, Rickenbacker and his crew survived on rubber rafts for almost a month.

"I AM THE LIVING BREAD THAT CAME DOWN FROM HEAVEN. IF ANYONE EATS OF THIS BREAD, HE WILL LIVE FOREVER. THIS BREAD IS MY FLESH, WHICH I WILL GIVE FOR THE LIFE OF THE WORLD."

JOHN 6:51

The men braved high seas, unpredictable weather, and the broiling sun. Night after night, they fought sleep as giant sharks rammed the rafts. But of all their enemies at sea, one was by far the worst—starvation.

After eight days at sea, all of their rations were gone or ruined by the salt water. They knew that in order to survive, they needed a miracle. According to Captain Eddie, his B-17 pilot conducted a worship service, and the crew ended it with a prayer for deliverance and a hymn of praise. Afterwards, in the oppressive heat, Rickenbacker pulled down his hat and went to sleep.

"Something landed on my head," said Rickenbacker. "I knew that it was a seagull. I don't know how I knew, I just knew." He caught the gull, which was uncharacteristically hundreds of miles from land. The gull, which seemed to offer itself as a sacrifice for the starving men, was something Captain Eddie never forgot.

In the winter of his years, every Friday evening at about sunset, Captain Eddie would fill a bucket with shrimp and feed the seagulls along the eastern Florida coast. The slightly bowed old man with the gnarled hands would feed the gulls, who seemed to come from nowhere. He would linger awhile on the broken pier, remembering a time when a seagull saved his life.

Jesus offered himself as a Sacrifice too. He is the Living Bread that came from Heaven. And just as Captain Eddie never forgot what one seagull meant to him, let's never forget what Christ did for us. Share the Bread of Life with those who are hungry.[37]

Christ is the bread for men's souls.

IN HIM THE CHURCH HAS ENOUGH
TO FEED THE WHOLE WORLD.

IAN MACLAREN

SWEET SLEEP

*A*re you a sound sleeper? Or do you sit up reading at your kitchen table late into the night? If you live near railroad tracks, you are probably used to the sound of trains and can sleep through the blaring of the whistle and the rumble of the engines. If you live near a fire station, you may be able to sleep through the sound of sirens. Some people become so used to the sound of their alarm clock that they have to find a new way to awaken themselves. Yet many people find it difficult to sleep soundly in stressful situations.

I WILL LIE DOWN AND SLEEP IN PEACE, FOR YOU ALONE, O LORD, MAKE ME DWELL IN SAFETY.

PSALM 4:8

The Apostle Peter probably was a sound sleeper. It seems that he could sleep soundly anytime and anywhere, day or night. The book of Acts tells us that Peter had been arrested for preaching the Gospel. Though his friends had gathered together to pray earnestly for his release from prison, things looked bad for Peter. He was chained in a dark cell between two guards. But somehow Peter managed to fall asleep despite the uncomfortable surroundings.

In the middle of the night, God sent His angel to rescue him. When the angel appeared in Peter's cell, the cell lit up with a supernatural glow. Yet Peter was such a sound sleeper that a light shining in his eyes didn't awaken him! The Bible says that the angel had to physically strike him on the side to wake him up. Once the angel had his attention, his chains fell off, and he escaped from prison.

We can be sound sleepers, too, despite hard times and stressful situations, if we learn what Peter knew well: God is in control. When we trust that God is in control of every aspect of our lives, we can "lie down and sleep in peace." Trusting in God's control is the best way to ensure sound sleep and sweet dreams!

WORRYING IS LIKE PAYING INTEREST
ON A DEBT YOU MIGHT NEVER OWE.

MARK TWAIN

A Perfect Recipe

AN ANGEL OF THE LORD SAID TO
PHILIP, "GO SOUTH TO THE ROAD—
THE DESERT ROAD—THAT GOES
DOWN FROM JERUSALEM TO GAZA."
SO HE STARTED OUT.

ACTS 8:26-27

story is told about a young bride who attempted to bake her first cake from scratch. The finished product was inedible, and the young woman sobbed her frustration to her mother. "I don't understand why it didn't look like the picture," she cried.

"Did you follow the recipe?" asked her sympathetic mother.

"Yes," replied the young woman. "I had to make a few substitutions though. The recipe said to use baking powder, but I only had baking soda, so I used that instead. And I didn't have baker's chocolate, so I used a candy bar. And I only had half the amount of flour, so I substituted extra sugar to make up the difference. And then Tom was due home early, and I wanted the cake to be done, so I took it out of the oven when I heard his footsteps on the porch. Do you think it needed to bake for more than fifteen minutes?"

What the young woman failed to realize was the importance of following a recipe exactly as it is written. The proper oven temperature and time and the exact amount of specific ingredients, blended in the right way, will yield a picture-perfect result. Anything less than complete adherence to a recipe invites disaster.

God has a recipe for each of our lives too. Our recipe will be a little bit different from another person's. One person may need more time in the oven of adversity than someone else. One may need more sweet experiences in life. Another may need the moisture of tears to soften a hardened heart. And still another may need more sunny yolks to brighten a dreary existence.

Only God knows the best recipe for our lives. Ask Him today to show you what He wants you to add to the recipe of your life, what He wants you to do, and where He wants you to go. If you follow His recipe exactly, your life can look just like the one He pictured for you.

A PERSON WHO LIVES ONLY
FOR HIMSELF NEVER KNOWS
THE REAL JOYS OF LIFE.

MOTTO FROM AN AMISH SCHOOL

A BALANCED LIFE

*H*enry tried with all his might to follow God. He attended church faithfully and served as a deacon. His mission, he felt, was ministering to the different families assigned to him, so several nights a week, he'd come home from work, take a shower, and leave to visit one of them.

I DESIRE TO DO YOUR WILL, O MY GOD; YOUR LAW IS WITHIN MY HEART.

PSALM 40:8

On other nights, he attended meetings at church. He had a part in every program and every committee that the church sponsored. He was a dedicated and well-informed man, so the church often looked to him for advice.

One night when Henry arrived home from work, his family was not there. He was appalled that his meal was not ready. How could he ever get to church on time if dinner was late? He went ahead and took his shower, hoping that his wife and children would be home soon. After another hour, they had not returned, so he finally left for his meeting.

When he arrived home later that evening, his family was already asleep. Upset, Henry awakened his wife and asked her where they had been and why dinner had not been prepared.

"We were at Keith's sports award banquet, Honey. You were supposed to be there, too, remember?" she replied softly.

Henry hung his head. At that moment, he realized that he had neglected his own family while he was seeking to serve others for God. Yet his family had been patient and understanding with him.

The following Sunday, Henry resigned from most of his committees, discovering that he was more effective with only one church-related responsibility. He had learned to serve wisely without sacrificing the most important gift of all—the love and welfare of his family.

THERE IS ONE GIFT VALUED ABOVE ALL
OTHERS, AND THAT IS THE GIFT OF ONESELF.

THERESA ANN HUNT

A CREATIVE BOOST

When Larry was a child, his mother followed a regimented schedule of housekeeping and menu plans. Monday was letter-writing day and meat loaf for supper. Tuesday was reserved for laundry and baked chicken. Wednesday was the day to help Grandma with her housework while a roast simmered in the oven. Every day had its own chore and its own menu. And, though it was repetitive, the family always knew what to expect.

Lisa, however, had been raised in an unscheduled environment. Her mother's whim, coupled with the food in the cupboard, determined what a given night's supper would be. When Larry and Lisa married, he wanted to know what she planned to serve for dinner every night. He was used to regularly scheduled menus and appreciated knowing what to expect. Lisa found such a schedule too confining; she wanted the freedom to be more creative.

They decided to compromise. Three days out of every week were

BE GLAD AND REJOICE FOREVER IN WHAT I WILL CREATE.

ISAIAH 65:18

216

set aside as pre-planned menu days. On those days, Larry knew what to expect for supper. The other four days were left to Lisa's discretion. Since she was a culinary novice when they married, that meant four days out of every seven Larry had to eat her experiments. Some were so bad they were inedible. But some were so good she still prepares them now, twenty-five years later.

Cooking and menu planning, along with many of the other responsibilities of homemaking, can become repetitive without the boost of a little creativity. Since God is our Master Creator, we can ask Him to show us how to be more creative in our cooking, in our housework, and in every repetitive area of our lives. It may be something as simple as eating our hot dogs and beans on the good china, but if we mix some of God's creativity into our everyday tasks, we'll find that a little "zippidee" in our "doo-dah" helps relieve the repetition every time!

SINCE WE HAVE LOAVES, LET
US NOT LOOK FOR CAKES.

SPANISH PROVERB

THE JUNK DRAWER

"Honey, where's that little hammer I use to hang pictures?" Carl yelled from the bedroom.

"Look in the junk drawer," Cathy replied automatically, as she stuffed laundry into the machine. She heard him muttering and shuffling through the bottom drawer in the kitchen.

"There it is. Hey, I forgot I had this!" he exclaimed.

Soon she heard her husband whistling and tapping a nail into the wall. Sighing, she pushed the drawer shut with her foot. They had been married for twenty-three years, and everywhere they went, the junk drawer went with them. She couldn't even remember when they didn't have one.

Need some tape? Look in the junk drawer. How about some nails? Try the junk drawer. Old keys, hooks, two-sided tape, pushpins, ballpoint pens, short pencils, and other assorted gadgets or parts, whose origin had long faded from memory, followed them from house to house. While some of the disorganized stuff was useful, much of it could have been thrown away long ago, and a few of the items could be downright dangerous in a child's hands. For years, they had talked about cleaning out the drawer and throwing a lot of it away. But that chore was always last on the list of other priorities.

It made Cathy think about her relationship with God. It was so easy to postpone her devotions or let the day crowd them out altogether. Yet she had to admit that she always had time for her favorite television shows. What was she storing up in her heart? Good things? Useless things? Even dangerous thoughts? It had been a long time since she had taken inventory of her life.

With a determined tug, Cathy pulled out the heavy junk drawer and set it on the counter, and by the time she finished going through it that Saturday afternoon, everything had been returned to its proper place or found a home in the trash. *Tomorrow,* she vowed, *I'll start on myself.*

ONE ALWAYS HAS TIME
ENOUGH, IF ONE WILL
APPLY IT WELL.

JOHANN WOLFGANG VON GOETHE

A LOT OF FRIES

"BRING THE WHOLE TITHE INTO THE STOREHOUSE, THAT THERE MAY BE FOOD IN MY HOUSE. TEST ME IN THIS," SAYS THE LORD ALMIGHTY, "AND SEE IF I WILL NOT THROW OPEN THE FLOODGATES OF HEAVEN AND POUR OUT SO MUCH BLESSING THAT YOU WILL NOT HAVE ROOM ENOUGH FOR IT."

MALACHI 3:10

Four-year-old Billy could hardly wait. In his small world, a burger and fries were pure heaven. When his father arrived home with the precious bag in hand, Billy was thrilled. It had been two whole weeks since he had smelled that luscious fragrance. He quickly tore into the sack and popped a French fry into his mouth.

"Billy, may I have one of your fries, please?" his dad asked.

Billy looked up at his father, an expression of disbelief and then horror crossing his face.

"But Da-a-d," he whined with convincing pain. "They're mine!"

His father looked at him with open surprise. "Billy, who bought you those fries?"

With his head down, he answered, "You did."

Ever feel like Billy? Like young children reveling in the abundance of their parents' resources, we turn to God and say, "But it's mine!" when He asks us to give. Our time, our talents, our money, our heart, and our love all have been given freely to us. It should be a pleasure—a real joy—to return a small portion of something that never belonged to us in the first place.

Imagine walking into a church and having someone hand you a hundred dollars. In the middle of the service, the ushers take up a collection and ask you to contribute ten dollars. Wouldn't you joyfully give such a small portion of what you had received? When God blesses us, it is a pleasure to return the favor. Sing, play, dance, write, and give back to God part of what He has given you.

He promises that when we offer a portion of it back to Him, He will "throw open the floodgates of heaven and pour out so much blessing that you will not have room enough for it."

As Billy would say . . . "That's a lot of fries!"

USE EVERYTHING AS IF IT BELONGS TO GOD. IT DOES. YOU ARE HIS STEWARD.

UNKNOWN

NOWHERE TO HIDE

"How did you know I was here?" Patty asked as she rested her head against the steel post of the bridge and swung her legs gently over the water below.

"Where else would you be?" her husband, David, asked. He stood behind her, respecting her need for space. "This is where you always come when your heart hurts. After three years, you don't think I know that?"

Patty beckoned him to sit beside her. "In a way, I'm glad you know." He sat down. "I come out here to be alone, but I don't really want to be alone. Part of me needed you to know . . . to search and find me. I wanted to know that someone cared enough to worry about how I was doing." She paused and said, "I guess that's silly, huh?"

WHERE CAN I GO FROM YOUR SPIRIT? WHERE CAN I FLEE FROM YOUR PRESENCE?

PSALM 139:7

David took her hand in his. "No, it's not silly." He said nothing else. He just sat there, quietly supporting and loving her, knowing she needed to be alone but not alone, separate but still loved.

Our Heavenly Father knows us even more intimately than our own spouse. When we try to run and hide from God's presence, He is always there—not as an intruder or an accusing presence, but as a loving Companion. He is a Friend who holds us even when we're afraid to look Him in the eye. His love knows no hiding place. There is nothing to run from if we belong to Him. So often He won't speak a word when we try to escape Him. He just waits, acknowledging our choices and loving us just the same.

Have you run away from your Father? He is there if you want to talk to Him. He knows your heart, and He wants to be with you. Even in the moments of aloneness, God is your silent Companion.

STILL WATERS RUN DEEP.

ENGLISH PROVERB

WHAT'S WRONG, HONEY?

> "EVERYONE WHO ASKS RECEIVES; HE
> WHO SEEKS FINDS; AND TO HIM WHO
> KNOCKS, THE DOOR WILL BE OPENED."
>
> MATTHEW 7:8

Phyllis will never forget the day God answered one of her prayers in a miraculous way. Pregnant and at home with her two children, she had no means of transportation. Her husband, Carl, worked on the road and was driving their only car. She had no idea where he was, and as much as they wanted one, they could not afford a cellular phone.

The morning was going well for Phyllis. Her five-year-old twins played in their room while she cleaned house. Around lunchtime, she heard a loud thump. Just as she got to their bedroom door, she saw one twin sail off the top bunk. They had been warned not to play up there, but their desire to fly was just too great. The first twin had landed safely, but the second broke his arm, learning the hard way that little boys can't fly.

Carl wouldn't be home for several hours, and since she couldn't reach him, she immediately called her father for a ride to the hospital. She cradled her screaming son while waiting for her dad. It then dawned on her that if she didn't write a note, her husband would come home to an empty house. But if he found a note, saying they were at the hospital, he would think something had gone wrong with the pregnancy.

Crying out to God, she asked Him to have Carl call home. Just as she said, "Amen," the phone rang.

"What's wrong, Honey?" Carl asked. For several seconds, she was speechless.

"How did you know something was wrong?" she asked.

"I just had a feeling," he said. After she told him the news, her father arrived. Carl met them at the hospital.

Phyllis was thankful that her line of communication to God was open and that He immediately relayed the message to Carl, saving them both a lot of fear and worry. That line is always open. But you have to call first! Today, sharpen your communication skills by spending some time in prayer.

A MAN WITHOUT PRAYER IS
LIKE A TREE WITHOUT ROOTS.

POPE PIUS XII

A Heart of Hospitality

*B*ecause of Jeff's profession, he and Rochelle relocated many times over the years. However, one of the relocations was memorable, not because of something that happened, but rather because of something that didn't happen.

Jeff was required to begin his position in a new city before their home was ready for occupancy. A woman from a local church heard about his predicament and offered Jeff the use of her family's guest room until their home was ready.

When they finally moved into their new house, Rochelle wanted to show her gratitude to the woman for her kindness to Jeff. She called and asked her to stop by for tea, apologizing that she'd probably have to sit on a few packing boxes but assuring her that she would be most welcome. There was a slight pause before the woman replied, "No, dear, I won't come over just now. I'll wait until you have things the way you want them. Then we can have a nice visit."

The woman was no doubt only trying to give her some extra time to settle in. But things didn't quite work out the way she thought they would. Rochelle never seemed to get things "the way she wanted them." Some of the living room packing boxes stayed in the dining room for a few months, as they waited for repairs to be made to the living room floor. Then when those boxes were emptied, the dining room disintegrated into a mess of wallpaper, paint, and floor tile samples for the kitchen. By the time those things were taken care of, nine months had gone by, and Rochelle was too embarrassed to re-extend her invitation of hospitality.

A hospitable person is gracious, cordial, and generous. Hospitality asks us to open our hearts to others, whether our homes are picture perfect or not. And when we refuse hospitality, we may be hurting the heart of a stranger. Let's keep our hearts open to give and receive hospitality. We're sure to find God's blessings—and quite possibly a friend too.

A GOOD NEIGHBOR DOUBLES
THE VALUE OF A HOUSE.

GERMAN PROVERB

Mama's Kitchen

"**M**a, how about whipping up some of those hoecakes?" Pa had shouted many times through the years.

Ma always knew what those words meant. Pa was hungry. She never failed to put down what she was doing to go to the kitchen to prepare something for him to eat. She was a remarkable woman who could turn even the smallest amount of food into a delightful meal. Once she tied her apron around her waist, she was transformed into the best cook in the world.

A CHEERFUL LOOK BRINGS JOY TO THE HEART, AND GOOD NEWS GIVES HEALTH TO THE BONES.

PROVERBS 15:30

As she stirred up the cornbread mixture, she hummed old-time Gospel hymns. The hot, black, iron skillet sizzled when she dropped spoonfuls of the mixture on the pan. Somehow those hoecakes were always perfectly round and browned just right. Ma always said that the secret was in the pan. But the real reason for her success with cornbread was the cheerful presence of God in her heart.

After the hoecakes were cooked and dinner placed on the table, Ma always thanked God for the food. And once the blessing was offered, she would start to hum those old tunes again. While the hoecakes filled Pa's stomach, Ma warmed his soul with love.

God always blesses those who depend on Him. Ma offered a little; God gave a lot. She taught by example that the way people live reveals much more about them than what they say. Ma was a shining example. We can all learn from Ma and the many other "grandmothers" in the faith who have gone on before us. When we rely fully on God, even the simplest tasks make life richer.

CHEERFULNESS GIVES HARMONY
TO THE SOUL AND IS A PERPETUAL
SONG WITHOUT WORDS.

WILLIAM COWPER

GOD IS IN CHARGE

**THE RIGHTEOUS CRY OUT, AND THE
LORD HEARS THEM; HE DELIVERS
THEM FROM ALL THEIR TROUBLES.**

PSALM 34:17

$\mathcal{L}$inda stood at her kitchen counter, peeling potatoes. None of her adult children could manage to get away to visit on Father's Day. She fumed as she cut up potatoes and dropped them into a pan.

When a friend had given her husband, Hank, two tickets to a Braves game, she had been elated. "Surely one of the kids can go with you," she had said. She called one son, but his wife was working that day, and he had to stay with the children. Their second son lived in another state, and son number three had other plans. She had not been able to reach their oldest son.

When Sunday arrived, they had just about decided to give the tickets to someone else when Doug, their oldest son, called to wish his dad a happy Father's Day. His dad explained the predicament, having tickets to the game and nobody to go with. Immediately, their son said, "I can make it. Since we're running short on time, why don't you just meet me at the stadium?"

There was a flurry of indefinite directions, and then Hank was off to the game. Ten minutes later, their son called and anxiously asked, "Has Dad left yet?"

"Yes, about ten minutes ago," Linda said. "Why?"

"My keys are locked in the front seat along with my wallet."

Promising to relay the message if her husband called, Linda hung up. "Lord," she prayed, "please be in control of this situation. Help Doug find his father."

Four hours passed before she heard from her son. "Did you make it to the game? Did you find him?"

"Actually," her son said, a ring of laughter in his voice, "I picked him up on a street corner. He looked like a lost and deserted dad. And yes, we made it to the game . . . and the Braves won. What a great day!"

When one thing after another seems to go wrong in our lives, it's good to know we have a Father in Heaven who cares about even the smallest, most intimate details of our lives.

FAITH IS THE FORCE OF LIFE.

LEO TOLSTOY

SATURDAY MORNING BAGELS

When the kids were at home, Saturday mornings were always filled with cartoons, good-natured teasing, and cereal spills on the carpet. Now that they had the house to themselves, Nancy and Garth preferred to go out for breakfast. Cereal and toast had been replaced by warm, cinnamon-raisin bagels, hazelnut-lite cream cheese, and cappuccino.

At first, their empty nest had been lonely, but after a period of adjustment, the couple had learned to talk about other things besides the children. Their favorite breakfast spot played classical music, and they always sat in the high stools near the window, leisurely reading the morning paper and planning their day together. They were more in love now than they could have even imagined when they were first starting out. But that's not how it had always been. Their love had deepened and matured, as they grew in their own relationships with Christ.

HE WILL CALL UPON ME, AND I WILL ANSWER HIM; I WILL BE WITH HIM IN TROUBLE, I WILL DELIVER HIM AND HONOR HIM.

PSALM 91:15

If your marriage seems rocky right now, don't give up on it just yet. God has a plan for your lives together. When you think you're going to break under the stress of kids and bills and in-laws, send up a prayer (or several) for help to get you through the day.

Marriage isn't simple, and it isn't always chocolate and roses. Sometimes it's getting up for a glass of cold water in the middle of the night when your spouse has a sore throat. Other times it might be holding a light as he works on your broken-down car in a chilly garage, or saying, "I'm sorry," first when you've hurt the other's feelings.

God hasn't promised in His Word that you will never experience difficulties. But He has promised to deliver you out of them all. Be encouraged!

SUCCESSFUL MARRIAGE IS ALWAYS A TRIANGLE: A MAN, A WOMAN, AND GOD.

CECIL MYERS

THE POWER OF PRAYER

Small children are often taught to say their evening prayers by learning a prayer such as "Now I lay me down to sleep." Although teaching children to pray is good, the "roteness" that is often learned can lead to the devaluation of this very precious and important time with the Lord.

Because evening is wind-down time, we may think our prayers lack the power and conviction that is available earlier in the day. However, prayer at any time of the day can have a powerful effect on our world. Consider the following:

THE PRAYER OF A RIGHTEOUS MAN IS POWERFUL AND EFFECTIVE.

JAMES 5:16

- Queen Mary said she feared the prayers of John Knox more than she feared all the armies of Scotland.

- John Wesley's prayers brought revival to England, sparing them the horrors of the French Revolution.

- Revival spread throughout the American colonies when Jonathan Edwards prayed.

Time after time, history has been shaped by prayer. The Rev. Billy Graham once said:

> I tell you, history could be altered and changed again if people went to their knees in believing prayer. . . . Today we have learned to harness the power of the atom, but very few of us have learned how to develop fully the power of prayer. We have not yet learned that a man can be more powerful on his knees than behind the most powerful weapons that can be developed.[38]

Matthew 14:23 tells us Jesus sought to be alone with the Father after what must have been an extremely taxing day of preaching, teaching, and healing the multitudes. Perhaps our prayers are *more* powerful when weariness causes us to drop the pretenses of "religious" language in favor of direct communication with the God into whose hands we've placed our lives.

Tonight, speak honestly and openly with the Lord about your concerns, and make your petitions known. Then cast the care of them onto Him and sleep in peace, knowing He is at work on your behalf.

PRAYER IN ITS SIMPLEST DEFINITION IS MERELY A WISH TURNED GODWARD.

PHILLIPS BROOKS

TRUE RICHES

*T*hey were married as soon as they graduated from college. They both were smart, attractive, and voted "most likely to succeed" by their peers. Within two decades, they had reached some pretty lofty rungs on the ladder of success: three children who attended private schools, a mansion, two luxury cars, a vacation house on the lake, a prolific investment portfolio, and the respect of all who knew them. If you had asked them what was most important in life, they would have reeled off a list of all they owned, the places they had been, and the things they had done. Success was sweet, and money made their world go round.

It will probably come as no surprise to you to learn that one day the bottom dropped out of this couple's life. They had personally guaranteed a business loan, assuming that their partners were as trustworthy as they. Not so. One partner embezzled nearly half a million dollars, and this Couple-Who-Had-It-All started down the road to becoming the Couple-Who-Lost-It-All. In the midst of their problems, the police came to their door late one night to tell them their oldest son had been killed in a car accident.

This couple discovered something vitally important in the course of putting their lives back together. A neighbor invited them to church, and thinking that they had nothing to lose by going, they started attending, eventually becoming regular members. To their amazement, they found they were enjoying Bible study, making lots of genuine friends, and feeling accepted for who they were—not for what they had in the way of material possessions. Their children also found a place to belong (no designer jeans required).[39]

Ideally, none of us will have to lose it all in order to find it all. In fact, our Heavenly Father wants us to live abundantly. Keeping our priorities straight—remembering to put God first and others ahead of ourselves—is the key to sweet sleep at night!

SUCCESS CONSISTS
OF GETTING UP MORE
TIMES THAN YOU FALL.

OLIVER GOLDSMITH

HEART'S HOME

Thoughts of "Home Sweet Home" don't usually conjure up high-tech images in our mind. But the new house of Microsoft CEO, Bill Gates, will have, not surprisingly, the latest in technological comforts and conveniences. When you enter his new house, you will receive an electronic pin to clip to your clothes. The pin identifies who and where you are and is programmed with your specific interests and tastes.

As you walk from room to room, the house adapts itself to your likes and dislikes. The temperature in each room automatically adjusts to your preference. The music you like will move with you from room to room. Digital images you want to see will appear on the walls of the rooms just before you enter, then vanish after you leave.

What happens if there is more than one person in the room? No problem! The computer selects programming that suits both of your tastes![40]

> LORD, THOU HAST BEEN OUR DWELLING PLACE IN ALL GENERATIONS.
>
> PSALM 90:1 KJV

Technology being what it is, some day we may all be able to customize our homes to respond to our most immediate interests, tastes, and comfort levels.

But there is something about the idea of "home" that goes well beyond the comfort and beauty of the physical surroundings. Home is a place where we can be ourselves. In that sense, there is a way in which no place on this planet will ever really be home for us.

George MacDonald in his work *Thomas Wingfold, Curate* said:

> "But there is that in us which is not at home in this world, which I believe holds secret relations with every star, or perhaps rather, with that in the heart of God whence issued every star. . . . To that in us, this world is so far strange and unnatural and unfitting, and we need a yet homelier home. Yea, no home at last will do, but the home of God's heart."

FROM QUIET HOMES AND FIRST BEGINNING, OUT TO THE UNDISCOVERED ENDS, THERE'S NOTHING WORTH THE WEAR OF WINNING BUT LAUGHTER AND THE LOVE OF FRIENDS.

HILAIRE BELLOC

NOT EXACTLY PUPPY LOVE

*A*aron and Abbey had been happily married for nearly a year when Aaron bought her a "present" she never wanted: a great big Chow puppy with paws the size of baseballs.

"Aaron, darling," she said with conviction, "dogs and I are natural enemies. We just don't get along!"

"But Abs!" Aaron used his pet name for her, hoping to soften her up, "You'll get used to him." It was pretty clear to both of them that the puppy was really a present for Aaron.

"Pup," as he came to be called, won an uneasy spot in their household. Determined that the dog should understand his place as her enemy, Abbey silently launched a campaign against him.

Pup sensed her resistance and reciprocated for a while by stealing towels, tearing up shoes and furniture, and carrying off whatever small object she was using the minute she turned away. He completely ignored her attempts to correct him. So went Pup's first year in the family.

Then one day Abbey noticed a change in Pup's approach. To her astonishment, he began greeting her joyously each time she came home, nudging her hand and licking her fingers in a friendly "hello." Whenever she had to feed him, he sat for a moment and gazed at her adoringly before he began eating. To top it off, he began accompanying her on her early morning walks, staying close at her side to ward off other dogs as she walked down their deserted road.

Little by little, Pup loved Abbey into a humbling truce. Today, she says that his persistence has taught her a lot about loving her enemies. She says Pup is winning—but don't tell Aaron.[41]

Is there someone you know—perhaps even someone in your own family—who needs an expression of your love, rather than your resistance?

ONE PARDONS TO THE DEGREE THAT ONE LOVES.

FRANÇOIS, DUC DE LA ROCHEFOUCAULD

SOLID ROCK

SEE, I LAY A STONE IN ZION, A TESTED
STONE, A PRECIOUS CORNERSTONE
FOR A SURE FOUNDATION.

ISAIAH 28:16

*E*ighteenth-century hymn writer Edward Mote didn't know he needed God until he was sixteen years old. Apprenticed to a cabinetmaker, he went with his master to hear a great preacher and was immediately converted. He was God's man from that day forward, but it took him fifty-five years to realize one of his dreams: the building of a church for his local Baptist congregation.

Grateful to him for being the driving force behind the new building, the people offered him the deed to the property, which he turned down. All he wanted was the pulpit, to preach Jesus Christ. "When I stop doing that," he told them, "get rid of me!"

Of the more than one hundred hymns he wrote, Mote is probably best known for "The Solid Rock." The chorus came to him one morning as he was preparing for work, and he had the first four verses written before the day was done. The following Sabbath, he stopped to visit a dying parishioner and sang the hymn to her. She was so comforted by it, her husband asked Mote to give him a copy. He did, but not before adding two more verses.

Struck by how much the song meant to the couple, Mote had a thousand copies of it printed and distributed. Today it remains one of the best-loved hymns of the church.

> My hope is built on nothing less
> Than Jesus' blood and righteousness;
> I dare not trust the sweetest frame,
> But wholly lean on Jesus' name.
> On Christ, the solid Rock, I stand —
> All other ground is sinking sand,
> All other ground is sinking sand.[42]

All of us are building something on this earth, be it a relationship, a career, or a physical structure. Each day we are wise to check our foundation and make sure we're building on the Rock who will last forever.

AH! FOR A VISION OF GOD!
FOR A MIGHTY GRASP OF THE
REAL, FEET FIRM BASED ON
GRANITE IN PLACE OF
CRUMBLING SAND!

RODEN NOEL

NIGHT LIGHTS

*A*n Illinois pastor had six couples enrolled in a new-members class that met on Sunday evenings in one couple's home. Even after all the couples had completed the course work and joined the church, they continued to meet on Sunday evenings. They enjoyed each other's company and developed a deep sense of commitment to one another.

One night, the pastor received a call from one of the wives in the group. Her husband's plane had gone down, and she didn't know if he were dead or alive. The pastor immediately called the other group members, who rallied around her. They sat and prayed with her until word came that her husband was dead. Then various women took turns baby-sitting and staying with her during those first difficult nights.

Group members opened their homes to out-of-town relatives who came for the funeral. The men kept her car running and did yard work. And when she decided she would have to sell her house and find a smaller place to

YOU ARE MY LAMP, O LORD; THE LORD TURNS MY DARKNESS INTO LIGHT.

2 SAMUEL 22:29

live, they helped her locate an apartment, pack, unpack, and settle into her new home.

For many people, this experience would seem like a night without end, a shadow on their lives that would never be erased. But because her friends let their lights shine into her darkness, they reminded her of the God who understood her pain and promised to see her through it.

"You are the light of the world," Jesus said. "A city on a hill cannot be hidden. Neither do people light a lamp and put it under a bowl. Instead they put it on its stand, and it gives light to everyone in the house" (Matthew 5:14-15). In a world that seems to grow darker day by day, let the Lord turn your darkness into light. Then you can brighten the lives of those around you by being one of God's "night lights."

WHAT SUNSHINE IS TO FLOWERS,
SMILES ARE TO HUMANITY.

GEORGE ADDISON

ENDLESS LOVE

The beautiful hymn "O Love That Will Not Let Me Go" was penned by a Scottish minister, George Matheson, who was totally blind. While he would never disclose what triggered the beautiful lyrics, it was widely speculated that his sister's wedding reminded him of a heartbreaking event. Just before he was to wed his college sweetheart, she was told of his impending blindness. She is said to have informed him, "I do not wish to be the wife of a blind preacher." Matheson gives this account:

I HAVE LOVED YOU WITH AN EVERLASTING LOVE; I HAVE DRAWN YOU WITH LOVINGKIND-NESS.

JEREMIAH 31:3

My hymn was composed . . . the night of my sister's marriage. . . . Something happened to me, which was known only to myself, and which caused me the most severe mental suffering. The hymn was the fruit of that suffering. It was the quickest bit of work I ever did in my life. I had the impression of having it dictated to me by some inward voice rather than of working it out myself.

Having experienced rejection from an earthly lover, Matheson wrote of a Heavenly Lover whose love is eternal and faithful:

O Love that wilt not let me go,
I rest my weary soul on Thee;
I give Thee back the life I owe,
that in Thine ocean depths its flow
may richer, fuller be.
O Light that follow'st all my way,
I yield my flick'ring torch to Thee;
my heart restores its borrowed ray,
that in Thy sunshine's blaze
its day may brighter, fairer be.[43]

The love that first drew you to God is the same love that now surrounds you tonight and will be with you forever, in all situations. Whatever you are going through, allow Him to comfort you.

HOW SWEET THE NAME OF JESUS
SOUNDS IN A BELIEVER'S EAR! IT
SOOTHES HIS SORROWS, HEALS HIS
WOUNDS, AND DRIVES AWAY HIS FEAR!

JOHN NEWTON

VITAL CONNECTIONS

AS YOU RECEIVED CHRIST JESUS THE LORD, SO CONTINUE TO LIVE IN HIM. KEEP YOUR ROOTS DEEP IN HIM AND HAVE YOUR LIVES BUILT ON HIM.

COLOSSIANS 2:6-7 NCV

The root system of bunch grass that grows in the hilly high country is deep, far reaching, and very extensive. A single plant may have up to seventeen miles of roots growing underground. This sturdy grass withstands the extensive grazing and trampling of livestock and each year puts out new growth.

All year round the bunch grass provides protein for animals. Even when covered by winter snow, it provides rich nutrition for deer, mountain sheep, and range horses. In the fall, its bronze blades provide one of the best nutrition sources available.

People also need vast root systems so their lives can be nourished and provide nourishment for others. Our root system gives us the strength to withstand being "trampled" by the challenges we face everyday, and it gives us the nutrition we need to replenish our resources when we've been "grazed" upon.

What makes up our root system? For most of us, it's family. Our parents and relatives began nurturing us the day we were born. No matter how many miles or years separate us, we turn to them (or to our memory of what they taught us) for wisdom and guidance.

Another part of our root system is people outside the family circle—our friends, coworkers, and people in our church, who have loved us, believed in us, and given us a helping hand as we've struggled to find our place in the world.

More important than all these is our vital connection to God. If your family, friends, coworkers, and church forsake you, God will never forsake you. He is the One who knows everything about you and still loves you. He gives you the desires of your heart and has shaped your destiny.

Let your roots grow down deep into the soil of God's loving presence, and He will provide you with nourishment that will overflow into the lives of all those around you.

FLOWERS ONLY FLOURISH
RIGHTLY IN THE GARDEN OF
SOMEONE WHO LOVES THEM.

JOHN RUSKIN

FORTY WINKS

*H*ow can young doctors be on duty nearly twenty-four hours at a time, day after day, and still be alert in a crisis?

Belgian researchers decided to do a study of hospital residents and the effects of their grueling schedules. Stress levels were measured after residents worked a twenty-four-hour shift that encompassed the emergency room, regular ward duties, the intensive-care unit, and a return to the ward at the end of the shift.

Although lack of sleep played a part in raising levels of stress-related hormones, the researchers concluded that a heavy workload on top of important responsibilities was the foremost factor in creating stress. Another way of looking at the research is to say, it's still possible to do an excellent job, even when you're exhausted.

HE WHO KEEPS YOU WILL NOT SLUMBER. BEHOLD, HE WHO KEEPS ISRAEL SHALL NEITHER SLUMBER NOR SLEEP.

PSALMS 121:3-4

NKJV

Have you ever tried to stay up for more than twenty-four hours? It's a near-impossible feat for most of us. Some scientists believe that sleep-inducing chemicals build up in the brain and eventually knock us out. But with certain jobs (such as being a physician) or round-the-clock responsibilities (such as parenting) some of us are occasionally called upon to pull double duty.

Rested or not, we have to be ready to jump into action at a moment's notice. We can do it—especially if we've managed to keep our normal workload and responsibilities within bounds.

In a medical emergency, it takes several people to perform all the ministrations required, and it requires shift work to be sure everyone is rested enough to do their jobs well.[44]

In your times of need, be willing to ask others for help. And above all, seek the help of your Heavenly Father, who never sleeps. He is able to watch over you and provide for you every waking—and sleeping—moment.

BURDENS BECOME LIGHT
WHEN CHEERFULLY BORNE.

OVID

THE SMALL STUFF

A man once said to his new bride, "Honey, I think the best way for our family to operate would be for you to take care of all the small stuff and let me take care of all the big stuff." His young wife agreed, and so they lived their lives.

At the celebration of their fiftieth wedding anniversary, the couple was asked to share their "secret" to a happy marriage. The husband relayed the agreement they had made as newlyweds. His wife added with a smile, "And I discovered that if I took care of the small stuff, there never was any big stuff to handle!"

Clearing away the small stuff of life—the daily decisions, problem-solving, and nuisances that need to be resolved—can be regarded as a burden, or it can be viewed as an opportunity to pave the way to peace and productivity. It takes just as much effort to remove small stones from a path as

"'THOU HAST BEEN FAITHFUL OVER A FEW THINGS, I WILL MAKE THEE RULER OVER MANY THINGS: ENTER THOU INTO THE JOY OF THE LORD.'"

MATTHEW 25:21 KJV

it does to arrange them so they make a better path. It's all in your point of view.

This prayer by Mary Stuart reflects a desire to move beyond the small stuff into the truly meaningful:

> Keep me, O Lord, from all pettiness. Let me be large in thought and word and deed.
>
> Let me leave off self-seeking and have done with fault-finding.
>
> Help me put away all pretense, that I may meet my neighbor face to face, without self-pity and without prejudice.
>
> May I never be hasty in my judgments, but generous to all and in all things.
>
> Make me grow calm, serene, and gentle. . . .
>
> Grant that I may realize that it is the trifling things of life that create differences, that in the higher things we are all one.
>
> And, O Lord, God, let me not forget to be kind![45]

When we handle the small things, we can move on to the greater things!

LIFE IS A GREAT BUNDLE OF LITTLE THINGS.

OLIVER WENDELL HOLMES

NOTHING TO FEAR

LET HIM WHO WALKS IN THE DARK, WHO HAS NO LIGHT, TRUST IN THE NAME OF THE LORD AND RELY ON HIS GOD.

ISAIAH 50:10

When we were kids, most of us enjoyed camping out in the back yard. Dad would help us put up the tent, and Mom would make sure we had plenty of provisions. With flashlights, pocketknives, and the faithful family dog for protection, we were ready to brave the elements.

What we didn't count on was the darkness. Those trees in the yard, so innocent by day, looked positively menacing at night. And we'd think, *What are those tiny lights that keep moving around and flickering off and on? What if we get attacked by a wild animal that just happened to wander into our neighborhood tonight?* And then the idea hits us: maybe we could get Dad to camp out with us!

Dad arrived with his sleeping bag and more provisions, without recriminations or condemnation. We fell asleep with no trouble at all. In our memories, the camp-out was a stunning success.

The world can be a scary place anytime there's darkness. Hard as we try to keep a stiff upper lip, sometimes we just have to say, "Father, help!"

The story is told of the Patons, missionaries who went to a forsaken island known for its cannibals and headhunters. In the early part of their ministry, Paton and his wife slept on the beach each night. The natives watched them from nearby bushes, but never came near.

Thirty fruitful years of ministry later, one of their native converts asked Paton, "Those nights you and your wife slept on the beach . . . what was that army we saw surrounding the two of you?" Paton, of course, had no army, but he knew beyond a doubt who the "soldiers" were and that God had sent them.[46]

The God who watches over "your going out and your coming in" (Psalm 121:8 NKJV) can be counted on to protect you from the darkness of evil. Trust in His power, His love, and His name to keep you through the night, whatever darkness you may face.

THE ANGELS ARE THE DISPENSERS AND ADMINIS-TRATORS OF THE DIVINE BENEFICENCE TOWARD US; THEY REGARD OUR SAFETY, UNDERTAKE OUR DEFENSE, DIRECT OUR WAYS, AND EXERCISE A CONSTANT SOLICI-TUDE THAT NO EVIL BEFALL US.

JOHN CALVIN

LISTEN FOR THE MUSIC

*G*eorge Gershwin was talking to a friend on the crowded beach of a resort near New York City when the joyous shrieks of voices pierced their conversation. Clanking tunes ground out from a nearby merry-go-round while barkers and hucksters shouted themselves hoarse. From underground came the deep roar of the subway; beside them crashed the relentless waves of the ocean.

HOW SHALL WE SING THE LORD'S SONG IN A STRANGE LAND?

PSALM 137:4 KJV

Gershwin listened and then remarked to his friend, "All of this could form such a beautiful pattern of sound. It could turn into a magnificent musical piece expressive of every human activity and feeling with pauses, counterpoints, blends and climaxes of sound that would be beautiful. . . . But it is not that. . . . It is all discordant, terrible and exhausting—as we hear it now. The pattern is always being shattered."

What a parable of our time! So many confusing sounds and noises, so much unrest, so much rapid change! But somewhere in the midst of it, a pattern could emerge; a meaning could come out of it.

Sometimes, finding the melodic line is a simple matter of listening selectively—mentally tuning out all but one sound for a while. That's what happens when we sit for a few minutes over a cup of tea and listen intently to that coworker, employee, or child. Once we listen and truly hear the "tune" they're playing, their unique melody will always be distinct to us, even in the cacophony of busy days.

If we are intentional about what we hear, the conflicting chaos swirling around our own symphony will be weeded out; God's music will be easier to hear.

In the midst of a busy day, it takes effort to hear all the melodies of those around you which make up the symphony of your life. But as each strain becomes distinguishable, a pattern emerges, and you can rejoice in God's unparalleled creativity in His world.

> ## OUR JOB IS TO HEAR THE MUSIC IN THE NOISE.
>
> UNKNOWN

GOOD FOR WHAT AILS YOU

"For God so loved the world" (John 3:16). Do you wonder sometimes how He can love all of us? Have you ever met anyone who seemed determined to be as unlovable as possible?

A woman who dearly loved her husband and son was having a very hard time loving her mother-in-law. The mother-in-law had decided that no woman was good enough for her son. She took every opportunity to remind the daughter-in-law of her opinion.

"MY COMMAND IS THIS: LOVE EACH OTHER AS I HAVE LOVED YOU."

JOHN 15:12

One day, the mother-in-law got the flu. She did not require hospitalization, but she was bedridden. Because her son's work hours prevented him from caring for her, he decided to bring her to his house so his wife could take on the responsibility.

Mom had the audacity to bring her own food, subtly implying she did not trust her daughter-in-law's cooking. Undaunted, the daughter-in-law set aside the store-bought food and got to work, preparing a mouth-watering pot of homemade chicken soup and a loaf of homemade bread. She served these delicacies in her best china, with the company-only, gleaming silverware, on a lace-covered tray.

Needless to say, Mom was shocked to be the recipient of such an elegantly presented meal. After several days of this service, her feelings toward her daughter-in-law softened. Although it was the dead of winter, the spring thaw came early that year![47]

If you have people in your life who have been a challenge for you to love, think of something extraordinarily nice you could do for them. Pray for them, and determine in your heart that, no matter what happens, you will love them as unconditionally as God loves you.

LOVE, LIKE A COOL, CLEAR WATER
SPRING, FREELY AND GLADLY GIVES,
REFRESHES AND ENRICHES.

WILLIAM A. WARD

PASS IT ON!

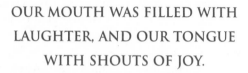

*O*n the first day of his cruise in the Caribbean, a man, entering his senior years, noticed an attractive woman about his age. She gave him a friendly smile as he passed her on the deck.

That evening at dinner, he was seated at the same table with her. To make conversation, he commented that he had appreciated her kind smile during his afternoon walk. When she heard this, she said, "The reason I smiled was that when I saw you, I was immediately struck by your strong resemblance to my third husband."

"Oh," he said. "How many times have you been married?" he asked with interest.

She looked down at her dinner plate, a slight smile crossed her face, and she tentatively answered, "Twice."

A smile is a great encourager!

An unknown author said it well:

A smile costs nothing but gives much. It enriches those who receive, without making poorer those who give. It takes but a moment, but the memory of it sometimes lasts forever. None is so rich or mighty that they can get along without it, and none is so poor but that they can be made rich by it.

A smile creates happiness in the home, fosters good will in business, and is the counter-sign of friendship. It brings rest to the weary, cheer to the discouraged, sunshine to the sad, and it is nature's antidote for trouble. Yet it cannot be bought, begged, borrowed, or stolen, for it is something that is of no value to anyone until it is given away. Some people are too tired to give you a smile. Give them one of yours, as none needs a smile so much as the one who has no more to give.

Have you been grumpy today? Ask God for a double dose of His joy and then put a smile on your face. Let people know you refuse to take on the negativism or cynicism of the world. You can be cheer-ful and pass that cheer on to others with a simple smile.

CHEERFULNESS OR
JOYFULNESS IS THE
ATMOSPHERE UNDER
WHICH ALL THINGS THRIVE.

JEAN PAUL RICHTER

UNEARTHING RESOURCES

*M*embers of a mountaineering club were planning to build a cabin in the mountains. One hot August afternoon they went out to the building site to look for a water source for the proposed structure. There had been a small spring at the foot of the hill where the cabin was to be built, but on that dry summer day all they found was a steady little trickle.

One of the club members thought the trickle was just drainage off the hillside and doubted if there really was an underground spring. Another climber noticed there was not just one trickle but several, which wasn't much proof of an underground stream. Still a third member thought they might find the stream but questioned whether it was large enough for a dependable water supply.

As unpromising as the prospect seemed, they found no other possible water source, so they agreed to begin digging. Shovelsful of topsoil were removed down to the sandy soil where the trickles got much larger. When they followed each one to its source, they found that all the trickles converged into a single underground pool fed by a spring.

The crew worked hard and quickly that afternoon, walling up the underground spring with stone and concrete to make a well hole. In less than an hour the well filled to capacity, holding fifty gallons. It would provide a reliable supply of cool, refreshing water.

People of all ages have looked in many places to find a fountain of life from which to draw the resources and strength required for living. Jesus said, "If any one thirst, let him come to me and drink. He who believes in me, as the scripture has said, 'Out of his heart shall flow rivers of living water'" (John 7:37-38 RSV).

IF GOD SENDS US ON STONY PATHS, HE
WILL PROVIDE US WITH STRONG SHOES.

ALEXANDER MACLAREN

STICKS AND STONES

*H*ave you noticed how a project can seem to expand? You break a job down into small parts and get most of those done, but during the day other elements are added to the mix. Before you know it, a straightforward task is out of control.

It's a lot like clearing a field before building a house. There are trees to chop down, roots to dig up, and rocks to clear away. After several weeks of digging, lifting, and raking, it appears the work is done and the land is ready. Then a major rainstorm washes away some layers of dirt, or a cold snap pushes more rocks to the surface. Your cleared field is suddenly dotted with rocks, stones, and sticks. And so it goes, often for years.

How do you cope with a field that won't stay cleared or a job that never seems to end? The fact is, most jobs do have a beginning, a middle, and an end. It helps to remember that![48]

Don't allow the interruptions and additions to paralyze your

IN ALL THESE THINGS WE ARE MORE THAN CONQUERORS THROUGH HIM WHO LOVED US.

ROMANS 8:37 NKJV

progress. The field is eventually clear enough to build the house, the report is put together, the test is completed, the results are analyzed, the product is manufactured.

The Apostle Paul knew a little bit about overcoming obstacles that threatened to make his job impossible. In 2 Corinthians 11:23-29, he outlines some of the hardships he endured in his mission to spread the Gospel: imprisonment, floggings, exposure to death, lashings, stoning, shipwrecks, lack of sleep, hunger, and thirst. Most believers would quit if a couple of these things happened to them, but not Paul.

Paul wrote that "we are God's workmanship"—a work in progress!—"created in Christ Jesus to do good works, which God prepared in advance for us to do" (Ephesians 2:10).

When we face a job with multiple components and no clear end in sight, we do well to recall that God can give us the strength to handle our own works in progress. The One who made us will give us all we need to complete every job.

GOD GIVES THE SHOULDER ACCORDING TO THE BURDEN.

GERMAN PROVERB

A MOMENT OF SILENCE

THE GOD OF PEACE BE WITH YOU ALL.

ROMANS 15:33

*T*he marriage is going through one of its "trying times." The kids are having trouble in school. There's too much month left at the end of the money. The roof of the house has developed an untraceable leak. The boss is making impossible demands. Wouldn't it be wonderful if you could run away from home—just for a little while?

A man named Alex was having difficulties similar to the ones listed above. His first inclination was to call his good friend Peter. Late one afternoon, during a walk around the lake, he poured out his heart and shared his pain with the person he knew he could trust.

What did Peter say while Alex unburdened himself? Almost nothing. He knew he couldn't wave a magic wand and solve his problems, and he was also wise enough to know that in some situations, saying very little is a better healing balm than empty words of sympathy. For Alex, spending a short time with a friend who simply listened was all the therapy he needed.

When Alex ran out of words, Peter's silence helped him to find a silence of his own—and some of the peace and quiet and stillness he so desperately needed. He also learned a lesson that day: how to listen to the people in his life.[49]

The American philosopher Eugene Kennedy has said: "We can master the art of being quiet in order to be able to hear clearly what others are saying. . . . to cut off the garbled static of our own preoccupations to give to people who want our quiet attention."

Thoughtful silence can help us find solutions, or it can simply remind us that for some heartaches, there are no words to express the pain or provide a quick end to the suffering. Better than words is the love of God and His never-ending compassion . . . characteristics expressed through His willing-to-listen children.

SILENCE IS THE ONE GREAT
ART OF CONVERSATION.

WILLIAM HAZLITT

Hippos

When we think of a hippopotamus, the word *graceful* rarely comes to mind. Rather, we are likely to think of the words *cumbersome, ugly,* and *distorted.* There is little to admire in the way a hippo looks or acts . . . or so we think. They seem to be large, rocklike masses, ready to tip over any unsuspecting boat that may pass too close.

Visitors to a new exhibit at a popular zoo are learning otherwise, however. A large glass aquarium gives them an opportunity to watch hippos from a different vantage point—under water.

They are surprised to discover that even with its short fat legs, bulky body, and oversized head, the hippopotamus is a very graceful, agile, and strong swimmer, capable of staying under water for long periods of time. The tiny eyes of the hippo are better adapted to the underwater murkiness of African rivers than to the bright sunlight. Indeed, the hippo spends much of its time foraging along the bottoms of rivers.

The main function of the hippo in the natural order appears to be that of "channel clearer." Hippos eat enormous amounts of river grasses that grow along the banks of rivers, thus keeping the river free of blockages that might cause floods.

Ugly? Yes. But hippos are gifted in unusual ways and have a valuable role to play.

Every day you will encounter people who may seem awkward, different, ugly, or without much purpose. Look again! God has created each element of nature—plant, mineral, bird, fish, animal, and human—to fulfill a specific purpose, and to do so with unique talents and abilities. There is an element of beauty, gracefulness, and goodness in everything He creates.

HAVE A HEART THAT NEVER HARDENS,
A TEMPER THAT NEVER TIRES, AND
A TOUCH THAT NEVER HURTS.

CHARLES DICKENS

YOU'RE ALL HEART

That twinge in your chest and that pain in your arm . . . is it just a muscle pull, or is it something more serious, such as a heart problem? If it is your heart, what caused the problem, and what can you do to fix it?

When you consult your doctor, one of the first things he or she might ask is what kind of stress you are experiencing in your life. Most of us would answer, "Too much of the wrong kind." After all, it's not easy to cope with each day's major and minor irritations, people who annoy us, and events beyond our control.

"COME TO ME, ALL YOU THAT ARE WEARY AND ARE CARRYING HEAVY BURDENS, AND I WILL GIVE YOU REST."

MATTHEW 11:28

NRSV

In our world, stress is here to stay, and many of us have heart problems, or we have loved ones who do. So how can we help ourselves?

Surgery and medication aren't always the answer. And, believe it or not, diet and exercise aren't necessarily the most important factors in restoring your heart's health. Studies have shown that having a spouse or other loved one to talk to and rely on, avoiding the traps of depression and anxiety, and having a sense that you can make a positive change in your condition can overcome the effects of even the most seriously blocked arteries.[50]

How often do we worry about things we can't do anything about? "Do not worry about tomorrow," Jesus said, "for tomorrow will worry about itself" (Matthew 6:34).

How often do we see ourselves as powerless? Remember what the Lord told Paul: "My grace is sufficient for you, for My strength is made perfect in weakness" (2 Corinthians 12:9 NKJV).

How often have we succumbed to depression and avoided contact with our spouse or a friend? Paul told the early church, "Therefore encourage one another and build each other up" (1 Thessalonians 5:11).

We each have a part to play in our own physical and spiritual restoration and in the restoration of others. With God's help and the support of our brothers and sisters in the Lord, we can have healthy hearts.

WHATEVER GOD CALLS US TO
DO, HE ALSO MAKES POSSIBLE
FOR US TO ACCOMPLISH.

UNKNOWN

A Pastor's Heart

GUARD WHAT WAS COMMITTED
TO YOUR TRUST.

1 Timothy 6:20 nkjv

A manager with a major corporation once heard a visiting preacher say: "If you have any type of supervisor's role in your company, then you need to have a pastor's heart. You need to minister to those people just as you would expect your pastor to minister to you."

The preacher made a clear differentiation between being a preacher of sermons and being a "pastor" to the people. He described a pastor as a loving shepherd who made sure all the sheep in the parish were nurtured.

The words lodged in the executive's heart. He had never thought of himself as a pastor before—far from it! His was a factory environment where tough discipline was expected from him . . . or so he thought. Nevertheless, the idea of having a pastor's heart was one he couldn't shake.

The executive began to think about what his own pastor did—visiting bedsides and funeral homes, conducting home visitations, and extending Christian friendship and concern. He decided that a portion of each day would be spent doing the same.

With increasing frequency, he visited relatives of his employees who were hospitalized. He made it a point to ask about family members and to show up at special occasions, from little league playoffs to graduation ceremonies. He began to encourage employees in as many ways as possible.

What he discovered was that morale improved greatly in his area of the factory, and along with it productivity and quality. In his own life, he found much greater satisfaction in managing with a pastor's heart than with an iron fist!

John Henry Newman once wrote:

> I sought to hear the voice of God
> And climbed the topmost steeple,
> But God declared: "Go down again—
> I dwell among the people."

IT IS QUALITY RATHER
THAN QUANTITY
THAT MATTERS.

LUCIUS ANNAEUS SENECA

EASY, ALBERT!

*E*ven the well-controlled temper can find itself sorely tested on days when nothing seems to go according to plan. As the shadows lengthen, occasionally the fuse gets shorter.

One young father with a new baby discovered a secret to handling his temper. Desiring to take full part in the raising of his infant son, he cared for the baby on his days off, while his wife worked a part-time job. On one particular day, his son seemed to scream constantly. The father thought a visit to the park might distract the child.

A WRATHFUL MAN STIRRETH UP STRIFE: BUT HE THAT IS SLOW TO ANGER APPEASETH STRIFE.

PROVERBS 15:18 KJV

He pushed the stroller along at an easy pace and appeared to be unruffled by his still crying baby. A mother with her baby strolled near them, and she heard him speaking softly, "Easy, Albert. Control yourself." The baby cried all the louder. "Now, now, Albert, keep your temper," he said.

Amazed at the father's calm, the mother said, "I must congratulate you on your self-control. You surely know how to speak to a baby—calmly and gently!" She patted the crying baby on the head and asked soothingly, "What's wrong, Albert?"

"No, no!" explained the father, "The baby's name is Johnny. I'm Albert!"

Albert had stumbled onto something that actually works better with adults than with babies and children. When others lose their temper or seem to be baiting you intentionally, practice speaking in your most calm, quiet voice. In most cases, your tranquil demeanor will help them to calm down. And practicing self-control in frustrating circumstances not only diffuses strife, but also lengthens your own fuse.

Hard to do? Sure! But try this: Allow the other people to finish speaking their thoughts. Then, before you reply, take a deep breath. As you exhale, say to yourself, *Jesus, I love You.* Keep it up every time you respond. The powerful name of Jesus can calm even the angriest seas of temper!

A SLIP OF THE FOOT YOU MAY
SOON RECOVER; BUT A SLIP OF THE
TONGUE YOU MAY NEVER GET OVER.

BENJAMIN FRANKLIN

HOME FREE

$\mathcal{M}$ost of us remember hot summer nights playing the game hide-and-seek with neighborhood friends. The goal was to reach a designated point and cry, "Home free!" without first being detected by the person doing the seeking.

Many of us play a version of that game on a daily basis, hoping to make it home without encountering more of the world's worries and pains. We want to arrive safely and soundly where we can be nurtured by family members or friends. Home is a place we like to be completely and delightfully "free."

"IF THEREFORE THE SON SHALL MAKE YOU FREE, YOU SHALL BE FREE INDEED."

JOHN 8:36 NASB

At home we are free to be ourselves—to talk, to praise the Lord, to show our love, to give, to receive, to relax, and to do what we like to do rather than what others demand we do. These qualities certainly make home an attractive place.

There are some, however, who consider home a place where they are free to dump personal frustration, free to express anger or hostility, and free to rule and reign as a bully. Such freedom doesn't quite make for a "home free" atmosphere.

To arrive home with a real "home free" attitude, dump the excess baggage of frustration, stress, and anger *before* you get home. That may mean taking time for prayer before you leave the office or once you are in your car. It may mean stopping by a gym to work out or staying at the office an extra hour to get your work done there rather than bringing it home.

A home that is "free" is a wonderful place. Freedom, however, must be guarded, cherished, and protected— not taken for granted or abused. Then, we can safely reach home base to joyfully declare, "Home Free!"

TO BE HAPPY AT HOME IS THE ULTIMATE RESULT OF ALL AMBITION.

SAMUEL JOHNSON

WHICH WAY IS UP?

"I WILL NEVER LEAVE YOU
OR FORSAKE YOU."

HEBREWS 13:5 NRSV

S ome years ago a speedboat driver described a harrowing racing accident from which he managed to survive. He had been nearing top speed when his boat veered slightly, striking a wave at a dangerous angle. The combined force of his speed and the size and angle of the wave sent the boat flying into the air in a dangerous spin.

The driver was thrown out of his seat and propelled deeply into the water—so deep, he had no idea which direction was "up." He had to remain calm and wait for the buoyancy of his life vest to begin pulling him toward the surface to know where it was. Then he swam quickly in that direction.

Life can put us in a tailspin at times, making us wonder, *Which way is up?* We can lose our sense of direction and the focus which keeps us on course. How do we recover our bearings?

The answer may be as simple as that discovered by the speedboat driver: stay calm and let the "upward pull" bring you to the surface. The upward pull in our lives is that which looks beyond our finite selves to the greater reality of God.

A grandfather was taking a walk with his young granddaughter. He asked the little girl, "How far are we from home?"

The young girl answered, "Grandfather, I don't know."

"Well, do you know where you are?"

Again, seemingly unconcerned, "No, I don't know."

Then the grandfather said to her in his gentle, humorous way, "Sounds to me, Honey, as if you are lost."

She looked up and said, "No, Grandfather, I can't be lost. I'm with you."

Our Heavenly Father never loses sight of us and never leaves us. As long as we remain aware of His presence and are sensitive to His "upward pull," we will always know which way is up!

WE CANNOT DIRECT THE
WIND, BUT WE CAN
ADJUST THE SAILS.

UNKNOWN

WE GATHER TOGETHER

*O*ne of the greatest pleasures in life is a home-cooked evening meal. What a relief after a hard day to sit down in the late afternoon at a table set with familiar plates and filled with bowls of our favorite foods! What a joy to look up from our places and see the loving faces of family or friends!

During a meal like this, we reconnect with those we love, unwind, and speak our minds with no fear of censure. It's a time to be our comfortable selves. For an Amish family in Illinois, however, it also became a way to pay a debt.

Nine-year-old Samuel was in a terrible accident. Mangled by a machine used to grind up corn stalks, he almost lost his arms and legs. It took twenty-eight operations to save his life and three of his limbs. His family was grateful for the medical treatment he received, but daunted by the six-figure bill. The Amish community usually helps itself in these situations, but this was beyond their ability.

The family's solution was to open their home to strangers each weekend. People came for dinner and left a donation at the end of the meal. After five years, about half of the medical bill had been paid.

More important than the money, though, was the emotional impact on the family and their visitors. Those who came to dinner were touched by the simple Amish way of life and the happiness they saw in their hosts. The family was overwhelmed by the number of people who were eager to help and by the encouraging cards and letters sent to them.

In times of need, we don't always like to ask for help. We prefer to give rather than receive, and we wonder what we possibly have to give during a crisis.

An Amish family gave of themselves—their home, their fellowship, and good, nourishing food lovingly prepared. Around a simple table in rural Illinois, family and guests alike received an unforgettable lesson in giving and receiving.

GO OFTEN TO THE HOUSE OF A FRIEND,

FOR WEEDS CHOKE THE UNUSED PATH.

RALPH WALDO EMERSON

THE BEAUTY OF
DISCIPLINE

The ancient Chinese art of *bonsai* (pronounced bone-sigh) has existed as a horticultural art form for nearly two thousand years. The word *bonsai* literally means, in both the Chinese and Japanese languages, "tree-in-a-pot." Practiced all over the world, bonsai is a sublime art where shape, harmony, proportion, and scale are all carefully balanced, and the human hand works in a common cause with nature.

A tree planted in a pot is not a bonsai until it has been pruned, shaped, and trained into the desired shape.

BLESSED IS THE MAN YOU DISCIPLINE, O LORD, THE MAN YOU TEACH FROM YOUR LAW.

PSALM 94:12

Bonsai are kept small by careful control of the plant's growing conditions. Only branches that are important to the bonsai's overall design are allowed to remain, while unwanted growth is pruned away. The bonsai roots are confined to a pot and are periodically clipped.

The shape of these trees is always as found in nature. Some bonsai have been known to live for hundreds of years, and the appearance of old age is much prized. The living bonsai will change through seasons and years, requiring pruning and training throughout its lifetime. And as time goes on, it will become more and more beautiful.

In truth, the bonsai would be nothing more than your average tree, but for the discipline of the artist. Giving constant attention to the direction of growth, trimming away what is ugly or unnecessary, and strengthening the most vital branches result in a work of art that brings beauty to its surroundings for many years.

In our own lives, it is that same discipline that makes the difference between an average life and one that brings joy and beauty to its surroundings. With God's Word as our discipline, we, too, can become works of art.

LET GOD PUT YOU ON HIS WHEEL
AND WHIRL YOU AS HE LIKES. . . .
DON'T LOSE HEART IN THE PROCESS.

OSWALD CHAMBERS

PAY ATTENTION

WALK IN WISDOM . . .
REDEEMING THE TIME.

COLOSSIANS 4:5 NKJV

$\mathcal{A}$ friend of Episcopalian Bishop Phillips Brooks said to him, "I have no time in my life for Christianity. You don't know how hard I work from morning until night. My life is so full, where can I find time for Christianity?"

Brooks responded:

It is as if the engine had said it had no room for the steam. It is as if the tree said it had no room for the sap. It is as if the ocean said it had no room for the tide. It is as if the man had said he had no room for his soul. It is as if the life had said it had no time to live. It is not something added to life; it is life. A man is not alive without it. And for a man to say, "I am so full in life that I have no room for life," is an absurdity![51]

Our society, like Brooks's friend, is obsessed with time. We try to stay "on schedule" and "be on time." On holidays, days off from work, and on vacations, we want to "make the most of time." Our usual lament is that there is just "not enough time."

There are two Greek words for the English word time. *Chronos,* where we get the word *chronology,* refers to measured time—the time on a clock; the days, weeks, and months of a calendar. *Kairos* time, however, means purposeful time, time which God has filled with meaning, the "right" time.

We have all experienced *kairos* moments—times when everything came together, times when it was "right" to make an important call, write a crucial letter, apply for a particular job, or have a decisive talk with a friend or spouse. These are moments when we gain insight or renewed perspective, see the bigger picture, and discern God's hand is bringing together the fragments of our life.

How do the ticking moments of the clock become filled with a sense of God's time? To turn *chronos* time into *kairos* time we need to "take time off" for reflection and quiet. Our resting is not passive inactivity, but an intentional commitment to pay attention to God in all the times of our life.

WISDOM IS THE ABSTRACT
OF THE PAST, BUT BEAUTY IS
THE PROMISE OF THE FUTURE.

OLIVER WENDELL HOLMES

LATE-BREAKING NEWS

*T*here's a certain amount of fear that knocks at our hearts when we hear a newscaster say, "This just in . . . an item of late-breaking news." Most of us would rather not have late-breaking news because, whether of a positive or negative nature, such news interrupts our lives. It upsets our carefully balanced apple cart.

Our spouse calls to say, "I'll be late," when we've made plans for a nice evening together.

We receive word that a loved one is seriously ill just days before our international vacation trip.

We are nearing completion of a major project when our supervisor announces, "I have some important information that needs to be considered or included in your report."

Such late-breaking news can send us reeling. What we need is a strong dose of adaptability and

HE IS THE LIVING GOD, AND STEADFAST FOREVER; HIS KINGDOM IS THE ONE WHICH SHALL NOT BE DESTROYED, AND HIS DOMINION SHALL ENDURE TO THE END.

DANIEL 6:26 NKJV

flexibility, coupled with an extra measure of courage. Author David E. Lilienthal once noted that the genius of America was its ability to make adjustments. "We are adaptable," he wrote, "and because we are adaptable, we are strong."

There is a strength that comes when we allow ourselves to bend without breaking, to adjust without panic, to make midcourse corrections without abandoning the hope of our final destination.

Jesus called His disciples to "follow" Him, but He didn't tell them exactly where He was going or what He would be doing on any given day. Jesus continually adjusted His course to accommodate others in need, and He challenges us to do the same. The good news is that, while circumstances and situations around us may be forever in flux, our relationship with the Lord is sure and fixed. He does not change. He is *always* our Savior, Lord, Teacher, Redeemer, Comforter, Counselor, Rock, and Lover of our Souls!

How important it is to remember that when late-breaking news comes our way!

BETTER TO BEND THAN BREAK.

SCOTTISH PROVERB

PLANTING AND REAPING

*H*ave you ever come out of the grocery store or flower shop and said to yourself, "Someday I'm going to grow my own vegetables and flowers"? Perhaps it was price, quality, or the frustration of standing in line to pay that gave you this urge.

Then "someday" finally came, and you found yourself on your hands and knees in the back yard—digging, fertilizing, planting, watering, pruning, and weeding. A small piece of land became a much-loved, well-tended oasis.

Have you noticed what happens when you garden? Yes, the joints ache, fingernails break, sweat rolls off of you, and your hands and clothes get full of dirt. But something happens to your spirit as well.

A couple with five children were very wise in the raising of their family. They decided to plant a vegetable garden. The children thought its sole purpose was to keep enough food on the table, but their parents had something else in mind. When a child was fretting over some problem or not getting along with the others, Mom or Dad would send him or her to the garden for a weeding break. By the time one of the parents arrived to check on the progress, the troubled child was ready to talk or had worked out his or her aggressions.

Taking a break each day to till the soil helps us regain our equilibrium. By putting us in contact with some of the basic elements of existence—sun, air, water, and soil—it removes us totally from whatever it is we normally do to maintain our lives.

A pursuit like gardening teaches us patience, redefines our definition of beauty, and gives us confidence in our ability to do something constructive. As we learn to care for something besides ourselves, we have more to give to others when we put aside our hoes and trowels and return to our "other" world.

One of the best places to go after a hard day of work is home . . . to the garden!

PEACE IS WHEN TIME DOESN'T
MATTER AS IT PASSES BY.

MARIA SCHELL

The "Off" Switch

THE LORD IS MY SHEPHERD. . . .
HE LEADS ME BESIDE QUIET
WATERS. HE RESTORES MY SOUL.

PSALMS 23:1-3 NASB

When you were a child, how many times did you hear a parent say, "Turn off the light when you leave the room"? Sometimes a brief lecture about the high cost of electricity or the importance of being good stewards of the world's energy resources followed.

There comes a point in each work day when we need to turn off the lights by closing our eyes or dimming the lamps. At the same time, we need to turn off the noise! Turn off the beeper. Unplug the phone. Shut down the computer. Turn off the television set, radio, or stereo. Close the door, and turn off the sounds of the hallway, the city, and the commotion in the next room.

Those who lived through the air raids of World War II have remarked with great consistency that the best sound in the world to them was the sound of silence— no sirens blaring in the night, no bombs bursting, no airplanes droning overhead, no sounds of families scurrying to shelters. Silence was precious beyond words. It meant life.

Today our senses are bombarded by more visual, auditory, and olfactory sensations than at any other time in history. At times we need to give ourselves rest and turn off the lights and sounds around us . . . even if we don't leave the room! It is then that we can hear in our hearts what is truly important.

The prophet Elijah knew firsthand the truth of this. While hiding out in a remote cave, he was directed by the Lord to stand on the mountain as He passed by. Elijah first experienced a mighty wind . . . and then an earthquake . . . and then a raging fire . . . and then the sound of a "still, small voice." Elijah went out and stood in the entrance to the cave, for he knew that this was the voice of God. (See 1 Kings 19:11-13.)

Be still and be a good steward of your resources. Allow yourself to enjoy a time of solitude and silence. Let the Lord restore your soul.

SOLITUDE IS THAT MAGICAL
TIME WHEN THE
IMAGINATION TAKES FLIGHT.

CHERIE RAYBURN

STRESS AND SERENITY

"*H*on," the petite supermarket employee said in her southern drawl, "everybody I know says they are *just worn out.*" She took a deep breath, brushed a wisp of unruly brunette hair away from her blue eyes, and continued checking groceries.

Stress has become a buzzword for Americans, especially in the last decade. At some point in our lives, we are all overcome with hectic schedules and perfectionistic tendencies.

In his article, "Confessions of a Workaholic," psychiatrist Paul Meier wrote:

Having grown up with an overdose of the Protestant work ethic, I was an honor student who was somewhat overzealous . . . I was a first-class workaholic and I was proud of myself for being one. I thought that was what God wanted of me.[52]

But later through the help of friends, the conviction of the Holy Spirit, and biblical teaching, Dr. Meier established new priorities. At the top of his list was: "Know God personally."

He observed, "I've learned to accept living in an imperfect world. Every need is not a call for my involvement. I have learned to trust God instead of myself to rescue the world. He can do a much better job of it anyway."

Jesus, too, must have been exhausted by demands placed upon Him. When He departed to pray in quiet solitude, He left a significant example for us to follow—daily.

God is a tranquil being and abides in a tranquil eternity.

SO MUST YOUR SPIRIT BECOME A TRANQUIL AND CLEAR LITTLE POOL, WHEREIN THE SERENE LIGHT OF GOD CAN BE MIRRORED.

GERHARD TERSTEEGEN

TOOLS OF THE TRADE

We see it as we walk along an ocean shore, where steep cliffs meet with the rise and fall of the tides. The splashing of sand- and rock-laden waves have cut away at the towering sea cliffs. Day after day, night after night, the continual lapping of the ocean water silently undercuts the stone walls. Then in one sudden blow the entire structure can shift and fall thunderously into the sea. On a daily basis, the wear and tear of water on sea cliffs is imperceptible, yet we know that every wave hitting the rock is washing away some of its hard surface.

We see the same shaping influence in another aspect of nature—trees that grow at the timberline, a harsh, remote setting. The extra resins that flow in the trees, as a result of the severe winds and snowstorms at the timberline, produce a grain of wood that has a rare and desirable texture.

WE ARE HIS WORKMANSHIP.

EPHESIANS 2:10 RSV

Such wood is sought by violin makers because it produces instruments of the finest quality and resonance. Fierce storms, the short growing season, and whipping winds combine to yield some of the choicest wood in all the world.

As we are subjected to the endless wear and tear of everyday life, we develop faults and cracks in our lives. In God's hands, however, those stresses and changes become His tools for shaping our lives for His purpose. As our lives are yielded to and shaped by Him, He creates within us the ability to resonate His presence.

The varied and often difficult experiences of life, given to God, are how He transforms each individual into something beautiful. The Holy Spirit can work wonders on the rough edges of our stubborn wills and hard hearts, conforming them to His own will.

Commit your life to the Lord again this afternoon. Trust Him to take all that happens to you—both good and bad—and make you stronger and wiser, using you in His great plan.

TOMORROW I KEEP FOR GOD.
TODAY I GIVE TO GOD.

FRANCES J. ROBERTS

"WE INTERRUPT
YOUR LIFE . . ."

**I WILL SING TO THE LORD ALL
MY LIFE; I WILL SING PRAISE
TO MY GOD AS LONG AS I LIVE.**

PSALM 104:33

*L*iving longer is supposed to be a good thing. None of us wants to die "before our time." We want to see children and grandchildren and sometimes great-grandchildren grow up. We want to travel, enjoy the homes we worked so hard to build, and do all those things we dreamed of before and after retirement.

Life doesn't always turn out the way we planned. Yes, we might be living longer, but so are our parents. And oftentimes, parents have major health concerns that require constant care.

As children we were the cared for, but somehow we have become the caregivers. We had our life compartmentalized, but the model has to be broken because Mom or Dad has doctor appointments, therapy sessions, or activities to attend at a senior center—and we are the chauffeurs.

Mom needs groceries and someone to cook her meals. Dad's house needs to be cleaned, and the lawn needs mowing. Mom is lonely and needs someone to sit and talk to her for a couple of hours. Dad needs help buying clothes. An adult child's life can disappear in the process of caregiving.

Take positive steps if you find yourself in the role of caregiver for elderly parents. It helps to have a friend you can visit with from time to time—someone who isn't too close to the situation. You need the perspective he or she can give. It also helps to find a support group of people who have learned how to care for their parents with wisdom and joy.

Start each day by saying, "I'll do my best today," and avoid criticizing yourself for not doing everything perfectly. Take care of yourself! You can't help anyone if you get sick due to lack of rest, poor nutrition, or stress.

Above all, make your caregiving an act of love and not obligation. Ask the Lord for His grace and His peace to surround you, and whisper prayers to Him throughout the day.

MAN IS BORN BROKEN. HE LIVES BY MENDING. THE GRACE OF GOD IS GLUE.

EUGENE GLADSTONE O'NEILL

Somebody to Divide With

At the turn of the century, a man wrote in his diary the story of a young newsboy he met on a street near his home in London. It was well known in the neighborhood that the boy was an orphan. His father had abandoned the family when the boy was a baby, and his mother had died shortly after he began selling newspapers.

All attempts to place the boy in either an institution or a foster home were thwarted because the boy refused each offer of help and ran away when attempts were made to confine him. "I can take care o' myself jest fine, thank ye!" he would say to kindly old ladies who questioned whether he'd had his porridge that day.

Indeed, he never looked hungry, and his persistence at selling papers, load after load, gave the impression he spoke the truth.

But the streets are a lonely place for a child to live, and the man's diary reflects a conversation he had with

MY GOD SHALL SUPPLY ALL YOUR NEED ACCORDING TO HIS RICHES IN GLORY BY CHRIST JESUS.

PHILIPPIANS 4:19 KJV

the child about his living arrangements. As he stopped to buy his paper one day, the man bought a little extra time by fishing around in his pocket for coins and asked the boy where he lived. He replied that he lived in a little cabin in an impoverished district of the city near the riverbank. This was something of a surprise to the man, and with more interest, he inquired, "Well, who lives with you?"

The boy answered, "Only Jim. Jim is crippled and can't do no work. He's my pal."

Now clearly astounded that the child appeared to be supporting not only himself, but also someone who was unable to contribute any income, the man noted, "You'd be better off without Jim, wouldn't you?"

The answer came with not a little scorn—a sermon in a nutshell: "No, sir, I couldn't spare Jim. I wouldn't have nobody to go home to. An' say, Mister, I wouldn't want to live and work with nobody to divide with, would you?"

IT IS OURS TO OFFER WHAT WE CAN,
GOD'S TO SUPPLY WHAT WE CANNOT.

SAINT JEROME

INVISIBLE WORK

*T*rees have specific seasons for dormancy—a time when the tree appears to be inactive and not growing. This season of rest comes immediately prior to a season of rapid and accelerated growth. During dormancy, the cells and tissues within the tree are being repaired and built up. This activity is invisible to the eye. The tree is quietly preparing for the vigor of spring.

Dormancy is one of the most important periods in the life cycle of the tree. It is how a tree becomes fit for the later demands of adding new wood to its structure and bearing its fruit.

FAITH IS THE ASSURANCE OF THINGS HOPED FOR, THE CONVICTION OF THINGS NOT SEEN.

HEBREWS 11:1 NRSV

The benefits of dormancy apply to people as well. There is a mistaken notion that to be effective we must always be active. But people also have seasons in their lives when God is preparing them for what lies ahead.

Not knowing the future ourselves, we often have to come to a deep trust in God during times when nothing seems to be happening in our lives. Inactivity must not be equated with nonproductivity— God is at work behind the scenes!

It takes patience and humility to get through a time of dormancy. Most of us desire to be productive at all times so we can "get ahead" in our lives. We need to recognize there are times when, unbeknownst to us, God has to work in our hearts to prepare us for our destiny.

We need to humble ourselves before Him and realize we didn't create ourselves. We can't know fully what it is we will need in our future. Dormant times call for us to wait on the Lord and trust Him to do His work in our hearts. We can rest assured He is preparing us for something great, in His timing and according to His purpose.

AND 'TIS BY FAITH, THAT EVERY
FLOWER ENJOYS THE AIR IT BREATHES.

WILLIAM WORDSWORTH

THE GOOD SOIL

> IT HAD BEEN PLANTED IN GOOD SOIL
> BY ABUNDANT WATER SO THAT IT
> WOULD PRODUCE BRANCHES, BEAR
> FRUIT AND BECOME A SPLENDID VINE.
>
> EZEKIEL 17:8

*A*n employee approached his employer and said, "I've had ten years of experience on this job, and I'm still making the same salary that I made when I started. It's time that I got a raise."

His boss retorted, "You haven't had ten years of experience. You've had one experience for ten years!"

Many of us feel that our lives could be described in the same way: one experience over and over again—or at best, boringly few experiences. When this is the pattern of our lives, we not only become depressed, but we also have no growth. Just as a garden needs fertilizer and nutrients to enrich its soil, we need the enrichment of activities and experiences to broaden our lives and stimulate our souls.

Joseph Campbell once said, "I don't believe people are looking for the meaning of life as much as they are looking for the experience of being alive."

How, then, may we enrich our lives? It must be intentional. Don't think that someone else can do it for you. There are multitudes of ways to get started:

- Take up a sport that you always wanted to play.
- Take your spouse or a friend out to dinner and the entertainment of your choice.
- Plan a trip to see something or someone interesting.
- Volunteer to do work that will help the less fortunate.
- Visit a friend that you haven't seen for a while.
- Get involved in a place of worship that challenges you.

Participate! Learn! Sing! Read! Praise! Listen! Give! Talk with your God! In experiences such as these, you will find the Source of all the excitement that you can handle.

EXPERIENCE IS THE
MOTHER OF TRUTH;
AND BY EXPERIENCE
WE LEARN WISDOM.

WILLIAM SHIPPEN JR.

A Servant's Heart

Work is over, and you're headed home, but first there are several errands to run. When the last stop has been made and you're pulling into your driveway, you marvel once again at the all-too-common coldness of your fellow humans.

Doesn't anyone smile anymore? you wonder. *Can't people help me find what I'm looking for without treating me like a nuisance? Doesn't anyone apologize for making a person wait or for giving bad service?*

SERVE ONE
ANOTHER
IN LOVE.

GALATIANS 5:13

The boss of a moving company in the Northeast has a philosophy we wish every person who serves us would emulate. Knowing what a traumatic experience it is to pack up and start a new life in a new place, he makes a point of letting his clients know he understands and cares about what they're going through. In the process, he has found it is just as easy to be kind as it is to be abrupt.

The best example we have of how to serve is the Lord Jesus. In Matthew 20:28, He told His disciples,

"The Son of Man did not come to be served, but to serve." Jesus' dedication to service was evident in all He did, from teaching in the synagogues and preaching the good news, to healing the sick and performing miracles.

"When he saw the crowds," says Matthew 9:36, "he had compassion on them, because they were harassed and helpless, like sheep without a shepherd."

Isn't that the way we sometimes feel at the end of a long, hard day—harassed and helpless? Don't we want someone to treat us kindly and lead us home? What a difference it makes when people treat us well!

The law of sowing and reaping tells us that what we sow we will reap. (See Galatians 6:7.) As we become more and more a servant of love and kindness to others, we will find ourselves being served with love and kindness in return.

THAT MAN WHO LIVES FOR SELF ALONE
LIVES FOR THE MEANEST MORTAL KNOWN.

CINCINNATUS HEINE ("JOAQUIN") MILLER

FAIRIE PENGUINS

*O*ne of the most interesting of all natural phenomena to witness is the nightly return of the "fairie penguins" to their rooks in the sand dunes off southern Australia.

These penguins, only about a foot in height, swim for days, even weeks, fishing for food. When dusk approaches, one or more groups of fairie penguins return home. As if the waves are spurting ink onto the sand, the penguins spill out of the surf, then gather together in tight clusters as if gathering the courage to cross the naked sands. They make a bold dash for the dunes, hopping up and over any obstacles they encounter, each penguin hobbling toward its rook on a well-worn, tiny path.

Once at home, each penguin greets its "spouse" at the opening of the sandy cave which they share. They peck at each other as if kissing. They usually mate for

BEHOLD, HOW GOOD AND HOW PLEASANT IT IS FOR BRETHREN TO DWELL TOGETHER IN UNITY!

PSALM 133:1 KJV

life, and they take equal responsibility for nurturing their young.

After the initial greeting, both of the mated penguins may move down their path, as if to "greet" their nearest neighbors with a friendly hello. Tiny clusters of four, six, or eight penguins can be seen "chattering" for ten minutes or longer. Before dark, all the penguins have made their way into the safety of their rooks, where they feed their young and spend a quiet night.

The next day, the mate that has returned stays behind to guard the rook while the other mate goes to sea. Like clockwork, the penguins again march to the water, hurl themselves through the crashing waves, and regroup beyond the surf line to form raft-like structures that will "float" the seas in search of food.

What a beautiful image of God's family these creatures provide for us, as they cheerfully live and work together in unity!

WEAK THINGS UNITED
BECOME STRONG.

PROVERB

LANDSCAPES

MY BELOVED BRETHREN, BE STEADFAST,
IMMOVABLE, ALWAYS ABOUNDING IN
THE WORK OF THE LORD, KNOWING THAT
YOUR TOIL IS NOT IN VAIN IN THE LORD.

1 CORINTHIANS 15:58 NASB

The landscapes around a home are usually very personal and reflect the individual taste of the homeowners. Making the outside reflect the owner is a unique talent landscape architects and novice gardeners have in common. Their work is so admired that friends and neighbors drive by, take pictures, and try to copy what these talented landscape artists create.

Landscaping is indeed an art, but it is also much more. These eye-catching scenes say something about the owner. They express the preferences of the owner, giving insight into what is appreciated and worth all that effort to create.

Most gardeners will tell you that even though they love gardening, it's still work. It involves investing money, time, and hard work to create the desired results. For the first year or two, a well-landscaped yard requires just about as much work as a new baby does. But, if you are willing to follow the directions, invest in necessary materials, feed and water the garden plants, and battle the weeds, you can expect a lovely garden. It takes preparation and commitment—and a lot of hard work.

The way we live our personal lives also expresses who we are and what we appreciate. It takes preparation, the nourishment of the Word, and constant attention to the weeds in our daily lives in order to create a beautiful and satisfying spiritual landscape.

ONE THORN OF EXPERIENCE
IS WORTH A WHOLE
WILDERNESS OF WARNING.

JAMES RUSSELL LOWELL

STUBBORN AS AN OLD GOAT?

artin Luther had a favorite illustration he used in his sermons:

> If two goats meet each other in a narrow path above a piece of water, what do they do? They cannot turn back, and they cannot pass each other; and there is not an inch of spare room. If they were to butt each other, both would fall into the water below and be drowned. What will they do, do you suppose?
>
> As it happens, one goat will inevitably lie down while the other goat passes over it. Once the walking goat is safely on its way, the other will rise and continue on its chosen path. This way, both get where they wish to go safely.

YIELD YOUR MEMBERS SERVANTS TO RIGHTEOUS-NESS UNTO HOLINESS.

ROMANS 6:19 KJV

There is a great deal of concern in today's world about allowing others to "walk all over us." But lying down to give way to another in order that both might achieve their goal is not the same as being a doormat. Nothing Jesus ever did could be considered weak and helpless. In strength and power He laid down His life for us. His example teaches us we must be willing to prostrate ourselves for others to follow His example.

Next time you come to an impasse with others, consider what might happen if you simply yielded your pride for a moment and allowed them to:

- speak their opinions,
- present their arguments,
- offer their ideas,
- suggest courses of action, or
- perhaps even make decisions.

Ask yourself, *Would this change the direction I am going in my life? Will it keep anyone from Heaven?*

Prostrating ourselves for the benefit of others rarely costs us anything, but it may yield great rewards, both now and for eternity!

PRIDE IS A FORM OF SELFISHNESS.

D. H. LAWRENCE

ACCEPTING SUBSTITUTES

$\mathcal{A}$ recently married woman moved to a small town in Wyoming. Clothing stores were in short supply and her busy ranch life left little time for the long trips to larger cities to shop. Her situation was made more difficult by the fact that she was a hard-to-fit size. To solve her problem, she began relying on a major store catalog that carried her size. The printed order forms sent by the store had this sentence at the bottom: "If we do not have the article you ordered in stock, may we substitute?"

Since she rarely ordered unless she really needed the article in question, she was hesitant to trust strangers to make an appropriate substitution, but she replied "yes," hoping it wouldn't be necessary.

This approach worked well until one day she opened a package from the company and found a letter that read, in part, "We are sorry that the article you ordered is

> NOW UNTO HIM THAT IS ABLE TO DO EXCEEDING ABUNDANTLY ABOVE ALL THAT WE ASK OR THINK, ACCORD-ING TO THE POWER THAT WORKETH IN US.
>
> EPHESIANS 3:20 KJV

out of stock, but we have substituted. . . ." When she unwrapped the merchandise, she found an article of greater quality worth double the price she paid!

On each order after that, the woman wrote "YES" in large red letters at the bottom of the order form by the substitution question. She had confidence the store would provide her with the best they had to fill her order.

When we pray to God, we are wise to add to our requests that we are quite willing to accept a substitution for what we think we need. We can trust God to send us the perfect answer because, as our Maker, He knows what will fit us better than we do. Because He knows the future in a way that we do not, He can answer in a way that goes beyond our highest expectations. Every time He sends "substitutes," we can be sure He is sending something much better than we could have ever imagined.

FAITH IS THE CAPACITY TO TRUST
GOD WHILE NOT BEING ABLE TO
MAKE SENSE OUT OF EVERYTHING.

JAMES KOK

It Is Well

YOU WILL BE LIKE A WELL-WATERED
GARDEN, LIKE A SPRING WHOSE
WATERS NEVER FAIL.

ISAIAH 58:11

The creators of two popular comic strips each took a year off from work because they found it harder and harder to come up with fresh ideas.

The writer of a popular female-detective series of books took two years to finish her last novel instead of the usual one year because she was having difficulty with the plot, and she wanted to get it right.

The star of a popular TV series asked to be let out of his contract after one season because the demands of the show meant there was less time to be with his family. When the well is running dry, you sometimes have to stop and let it rest.

Some people are gifted enough (or stubborn enough) to push themselves to their creative limits for weeks, months, or years on end. Some of them burn out at an early age or even die early from single-minded devotion to their work. Others, however, seem to go on forever.

How do those who continue do it? By pulling back now and then . . . by always keeping something in reserve . . . by knowing when to slow down or stop, if only for a brief time. They know the importance of keeping water in the well.

In our work, we sometimes "dry up" creatively. We assume our own wells of inspiration will always be full, so we don't bother to take opportunities to read, travel, attend performances, visit galleries, explore new places, or do other things that feed our creativity. We each need to take enough breaks from our work to receive input from others, especially those who have valuable lessons or skills to teach us.

Instead of sending our buckets down into the same well over and over again, let's leave them above ground now and then and allow our wells to be refilled.

REST IS NOT QUITTING
THE BUSY CAREER,
REST IS THE FITTING
OF SELF TO ITS SPHERE.

JOHN SULLIVAN DWIGHT

REFERENCES

Unless otherwise indicated, all Scripture quotations are taken from the *Holy Bible, New International Version*®. NIV®. Copyright © 1973, 1978, 1984 by International Bible Society. Used by permission of Zondervan Publishing House. All rights reserved.

Scripture quotations marked KJV are taken from the *King James Version* of the Bible.

Scriptures marked NCV are quoted from *The Holy Bible, New Century Version,* copyright © 1987, 1988, 1991 by Word Publishing, Dallas, Texas 75039. Used by permission.

Scripture quotations marked THE MESSAGE are taken from *The Message,* copyright © by Eugene H. Peterson, 1993, 1994, 1995, 1996. Used by permission of NavPress Publishing Group.

Scripture quotations marked CEV are taken from the *Contemporary English Version,* copyright © 1991, 1992, 1995 by the American Bible Society. Used by permission.

Scripture quotations marked NKJV are taken from *The New King James Version.* Copyright © 1979, 1980, 1982, Thomas Nelson, Inc.

Scripture quotations marked RSV are taken from *The Revised Standard Version Bible,* copyright © 1946, Old Testament section copyright © 1952 by the Division of Christian Education of the National Council of the Churches of Christ in the United States of America. Used by permission.

Scripture quotations marked AMP are taken from *The Amplified Bible. Old Testament* copyright © 1965, 1987 by Zondervan Corporation, Grand Rapids, Michigan. *New Testament* copyright © 1958, 1987 by The Lockman Foundation, La Habra, California. Used by permission.

Scripture quotations marked NASB are taken from the *New American Standard Bible.* Copyright © The Lockman Foundation 1960, 1962, 1963, 1968, 1971, 1972, 1973, 1975, 1977, 1995. Used by permission.

Verses marked TLB are taken from *The Living Bible* © 1971. Used by permission of Tyndale House Publishers, Inc., Wheaton, Illinois 60189. All rights reserved.

Scripture quotations marked NRSV are from the *New Revised Standard Version* of the Bible, copyright © 1989 by The Division of Christian Education of the National Council of the Churches of Christ in the USA. Used by permission. All rights reserved.

ENDNOTES

[1] (pp. 6-7) Eleanor Farjeon, "Morning Has Broken," *The United Methodist Hymnal* (Nashville, TN: The United Methodist Publishing House,1989) p. 145.

[2] (pp. 8-9) *The New Dictionary of Thoughts,* Tryon Edwards, ed. (NY: Standard Book Company, 1963) p. 506.

[3] (p. 9) Richard Blanchard, "Fill My Cup, Lord," Chorus Book (Dallas, TX: Word, Inc., 1971).

[4] (pp. 12-13) *Book of Prayers,* Robert Van de Weyer, ed. (NY: Harper Collins, 1993) p. 67.

[5] (pp. 16-17) Toyohiko Kagawa and other Japanese Poets, *Songs from the Land of Dawn,* Lois J. Erickson, trans. (NY: Friendship Press, 1949) pp. 20-21.

[6] (pp. 24-25) Philip E. Howard Jr., *New Every Morning* (Grand Rapids, MI: Zondervan, 1969) pp. 12-13.

[7] (p. 42) *San Luis Obispo Telegraph-Tribune* (January 31, 1996) B-3.

[8] (p. 52) Reuben P. Job and Norman Shawchuck, *A Guide to Prayer* (Nashville, TN: The Upper Room, 1983) p. 176.

[9] (pp. 56-57) *Illustrations Unlimited,* James Hewett, ed. (Wheaton, IL: Tyndale House, 1988) p. 159.

[10] (pp. 62-63) Charles R. Swindoll, *The Finishing Touch* (Dallas, TX: Word Publishing, 1994) pp. 186-187.

[11] (pp. 64-65) *Reader's Digest* (December 1992) pp. 101-104.

[12] (pp. 84-85) *Good Housekeeping* (February 1996) p. 20.

[13] (pp. 86-87) *JAMA* (December 6, 1995) p. 21.

[14] (pp. 92) *The Treasure Chest,* Brian Culhane, ed. (San Francisco: Harper, 1995) p. 162.

[15] (pp. 96-97) *Illustrations Unlimited,* James S. Hewett, ed. (Wheaton, IL: Tyndale House, 1988) pp. 15,18,279-280.

[16] (pp. 100-101) Walter B. Knight, *Knight's Master Book of 4,000 Illustrations* (Grand Rapids, MI: William B. Eerdmans Publishing Co., 1956) p. 71.

[17] (pp. 102-103) *Newsweek* (March 6, 1995) pp. 60-61.

[18] (pp. 106-107) *The Treasure Chest,* Brian Culhane, ed. (San Francisco: Harper, 1995) p. 176.

[19] (pp. 112-113) *Scientific American* (August 1995) pp. 70-77.

[20] (pp. 118-119) Kovachevich Radomir.

[21] (p. 138) Jean Shepherd, "The Endless Streetcar Ride into the Night, and the Tinfoil Noose," *The Riverside Reader,* Vol. 1 (Boston: Houghton Mifflin Company, 1985) p. 32.

[22] (p. 138) Ibid., p. 37.

[23] (p. 139) Ibid.

[24] (p. 142) Robert Frost, "Mending Walls," *Writing for Change: A Community Reader* (San Francisco: McGraw-Hill, Inc, 1995) pp. 123-124.

[25] (p. 144) George Sweeting, *Who Said That?* (Chicago: Moody Press, 1995).

[26] (p. 148) Doug Lipman, The Hasidic Stories Home Page *(http://hasidic.storypower.com),* 1996.

[27] (p. 150-151) G. Peter Fleck, *Come As You Are*

[28] (p. 153) George Sweeting, *Who Said That?* (Chicago: Moody Press, 1995).

[29] (p. 155) Chorus by Mary Maxwell, Score by Ada Rose Gibbs.

[30] (pp. 174-175) Charles R. Swindoll, *Seasons of Life* (Portland, OR: Multnomah Press, 1983).

[31] (p. 183) George Sweeting, *Who Said That?* (Chicago: Moody Press, 1995).

[32] (p. 184) Jim Cymbala with Dean Merrill, *Fresh Wind, Fresh Fire* (Grand Rapids, MI: Zondervan Publishing House, 1997).

[33] (pp. 186-187) Shirley Monty, *May's Boy* (Thomas Nelson Publishers, 1981).

[34] (p. 188) Charles R. Swindoll, *Seasons of Life* (Portland OR: Multnomah Press, 1983).

[35] (p. 192) *Today in the Word* (September 25, 1992).

[36] (pp. 202-203) Jennifer Loven, *Dallas Morning News* (August 26, 1994).

[37] (pp. 208-209) Nanette Thorsen-Snipes, *Power for Living* (April 1992).

[38] (p. 235) Billy Graham, *Unto the Hills: A Devotional Treasury* (Waco, TX: Word Books, 1986) p. 130.

[39] (pp. 236-237) *Decision* (March 1996) p. 33.

[40] (p. 238) *Newsweek* (November 27, 1995) pp. 62-63.

[41] (pp. 240-241) *A Moment a Day,* Mary Beckwith and Kathi Mills, ed. (Ventura, CA: Regal Books, 1988) p. 247.

[42] (pp. 242-243) Kenneth W. Osbeck, *101 More Hymn Stories* (Grand Rapids, MI: Kregel Publications, 1985) pp. 274-277.

[43] (pp. 246-247) Kenneth W. Osbeck, *Amazing Grace* (Grand Rapids, MI: Kregel Publications, 1993) p. 49.

[44] (pp. 250-251) *Creative Living* (Summer 1993) p. 26.

[45] (p. 253) *The Treasure Chest,* Brian Culhane, ed. (San Francisco: HarperCollins, 1995) p. 109.

[46] (pp. 254-255) Ron Mehl, *God Works the Night Shift* (Sisters, OR: Multnomah Books, 1994) pp. 132- 133.

[47] (pp. 258-259) *Guideposts* (March 1996) pp. 10-13.

[48] (p. 264) Gordon MacDonald, *Ordering Your Private World* (Nashville, TN: Thomas Nelson Publishers, 1984, 1985) pp. 152-153.

[49] (pp. 266-267) *Decision* (October 1995) p. 42.

[50] (p. 270) *Psychology Today* (November/December 1994) p. 16.

[51] (p. 284) *Weavings* (January-February 1991) pp. 7-13.

[52] (p. 292) Paul Meier, M.D., "Confessions of a Workaholic," *The Physician* (March/April 1990).

Additional copies of this book and other titles
in the *Quiet Moments with God Devotional* series
are available from your local bookstore.

Quiet Moments with God

Quiet Moments with God for Mothers

Quiet Moments with God for Women

If you have enjoyed this book, or if it has
impacted your life, we would like to hear from you.

Please contact us at:

Honor Books
Department E
P.O. Box 55388
Tulsa, Oklahoma 74155

Or, by e-mail at info@honorbooks.com

Tulsa, Oklahoma